The Burning of a Strange Fire

Forty Years in Mormonism

by BARNEY R. FULLER

HUNTINGTON HOUSE PUBLISHERS

Huntington House Publishers
P.O. Box 53788
Lafayette, Louisiana 70505

Library of Congress Card Catalog Number 93-78567
ISBN 1-56384-049-9

Dedication

❖

To my dad, Connie Fuller, who was a Mormon elder for many years; a man whom I loved and admired so very much. In the last several years of his life, he became aware of the illusions of Mormonism in which he had once believed. He ceased preaching the importance of a church institution and found the great joy of sharing Jesus. He was a man any son would have been proud to say, "Yes, he's my dad."

Contents

———————— ❖ ————————

Preface

❖

This book has been written for the purpose of taking an in depth look into the roots of a religion I once held very dear to my heart. There yet remains in this religion many relatives of mine and many friends, all of whom I love.

I learned a long time ago that there are no religious walls that can restrain the faith of any person when they possess a genuine desire to know the truth. Such a desire will readily motivate a response from God. Jesus taught that it would. "But the hour cometh, and now is, when the true worshippers shall worship the Father in spirit and in truth: for the Father seeketh such to worship Him" (John 4:23).

The Lord is always waiting for our hearts to manifest a pure and sincere desire to know the Truth. God wants above all that His Creation have in their hearts His Word of understanding concerning all things. For us not to have such a desire leaves us loving darkness more than light. But this we do not have to fear, when we have a yearning within to know the Truth. Because ". . . he that doeth Truth cometh to the Light" (John 3:21). Light brings order to chaos, healing to the sick, and deliverance to the captives. The light of Truth brings us into communion with God, where peace passes understanding and our joy becomes unspeakable and full of glory.

Jesus could not have placed greater significance upon Truth than when He called the Spirit of God the Spirit of

Truth in John 14:17. And to each follower of Jesus, the Spirit of Truth would come to indwell them. "Howbeit, when HE, the Spirit of Truth is come, He will guide you into all Truth; . . . (John 16:13)." This Spirit will in the process of time lead the man of Christ to prove all things and hold fast to that which is good. He will be led to "renounce the hidden things of dishonesty, and to not walk in craftiness, nor handle the Word of God deceitfully" (II Corinthians 4:2).

When we are moved within by a desire to bring everything to the light, then all that is deceitful will be exposed and the bondage of its deception broken. But when religions are born upon deceit, then its followers are subjected to the spirits which oversaw the deception. To dispel such spirits and to break the curses of blindness and prejudice they have brought, we must call upon the One who is the light and who is mighty to save. His faithful promise to us is, "If ye continue in My Word, then are ye My Disciples indeed: And ye shall know the truth, and the Truth shall set you free" (John 8:31-32).

I am a fourth generation Mormon. My heritage goes back into the previous century. My great grandfather, Marion Fuller, was a Mormon priest. There is, also, another side of this heritage which focuses upon the first two founders of the Mormon Church. These two men were Joseph Smith and Oliver Cowdery. Both of these men carried in their veins Fuller blood, making them distant relatives of mine. The Fuller line which tied Joseph Smith and Oliver Cowdery together sprang from the line of John Fuller. The same Fuller line from which my family was to descend.

The Mormons have carefully concealed the knowledge that the Joseph Smith and Oliver Cowdery families were relatives. The family ties of the Smiths and Cowderys were much closer than the Mormons have been willing to tell. Mormon history portrays Oliver Cowdery as a "stranger" when he and Smith first met, but as the reader will learn, this was not the case.

I was baptized a Mormon in 1943, ordained to both of its priesthoods, attended one of its colleges and strongly believed its doctrines, particularly that Joseph Smith was specially chosen to bring forth the Book of Mormon and that he was personally called by God to be the great prophet who was preordained to usher in the last dispensation of times. I fully accepted, along with all Mormons, that Joseph Smith had been given the Keys of Divine Authority to bring forth and establish the only true and living Church upon the face of the earth. I further believed that the *Doctrine and Covenants* which contained Smith's revelations was also equal in scriptural authority to the Holy Bible.

Several years would pass before I learned that Smith had altered many of his first revelations. This was indeed shocking and disheartening to see with my own eyes where "Our Prophet" had committed such an act. Then as most Mormons do, we explain to ourselves that there had to be some justified reason for this. But I could find none, and soon I was wanting to see what was under every stone that Mormonism was founded upon. Thus began a very thorough investigation of Joseph Smith, a man whom in my mind ranked along side Moses and Elijah.

I was to find that Mormonism could not withstand a careful eye of scrutiny. Eventually, I was to carefully re-evaluate all that I had once accepted by faith and had so convincingly believed. My search would finally conclude with a full renunciation of Mormonism, and Joseph Smith as a true prophet of God.

Joseph Fielding Smith, one of the Mormon Prophet Leaders, strongly affirmed the following,

> The Church . . . must stand or fall on the story of Joseph Smith. He was either a prophet of God, divinely called . . . or he was one of the biggest frauds this world has ever seen. There is no middle ground . . . If Joseph Smith was a deceiver, who willfully attempted to mislead the people, then he should be exposed; his claims should be refuted, and his doctrines shown to be false . . . The doctrines of false teachers will not stand the test when tried by the accepted standards of measurement, the scriptures (*Doctrines of Salvation*, Vol. 1, p. 188).

This statement is like so much other Mormon rhetoric, cunningly devised words to present a proper image. When there has ever been a serious campaign within Mormonism to judge Joseph Smith by the scriptures, it has always been squelched by the Mormon Leadership.

The story of many Christian churches can tell it like it happened. They have nothing to hide. But this is not true of Mormonism. The true birth of this religion holds little resemblance to the story that they tell, as well as what they publish and teach to their own people. The spirit which led Joseph Smith to falsify much of his history is still inspiring a great portion of the Mormon writers today. This is seen in their unwillingness to openly tell the whole truth concerning those first years which were so crucial in the formation of the Mormon religion.

In this book the reader will be able to examine, as well as to witness that Mormonism was, from its inception, the offering up of a "strange fire" before the Lord, of which He did not command (Leviticus 10:1).

Acknowledgment

❖

To my wife, Joanne, who gave so much of her time in researching and critiquing everything, and for the many hours she spent at the computer.

And most of all for her patience in deciphering my handwriting. When she finished her reply was, "I enjoyed it all."

To Gary, my son, who assisted his mother at the computer, and gave up his time to make the final corrections for the publisher's copy.

Introduction

❖

Who Is Barney R. Fuller

I was born the son of a Mormon pastor on 21 May 1935 in West Monroe, Louisiana. In 1961 I graduated from college with majors in religion and physical education. In the year of 1958 I was ordained to the Melchizedek priesthood. Occupying this office of priesthood qualified me for Mormon ministry in various places throughout the ensuing years. During this same period of time I was to teach school both in Illinois and in California. While living in California I founded a non-profit organization called World Redemption. This organization would publish a religious newspaper for seven years. I would eventually be excommunicated from Mormonism in 1974, but I continued my version of this religion until 1978. At that time I broke all ties with the Mormon faith.

During the past twenty years, I have served as a pastor and as an assistant in the states of Missouri and Texas. In 1981 I began a company of my own which today manufactures products and distributes them throughout the United States. I continue to provide ministry as the opportunity presents itself.

I married a Mormon girl from Ohio in 1956, and we presently have three children and five grandchildren. Our

youngest son this year will be attending Southwestern As-
semblies of God College in Waxahachie, Texas.

We have many friends with whom we have been instrumental in assisting from the bondage of Mormonism. Many
of these are presently engaged in ministries seeking to lead
Mormons to Jesus. Several of these are eagerly awaiting the
publication of *The Burning of a Strange Fire*.

I have spoken and lectured in many states of the country. My travels have taken me into forty-nine of the fifty
states on a number of occasions. My wife and I over the past
thirty-five years have made our home in seven of these states.

Why I Have Written This Book

Most anti-Mormon writings have dealt with the fruits of
that religion, with little or no attention given to the historical
causes which authored the religion itself. This book's main
objective is to take the reader behind the scenes of Mormon
history, where words are spoken, acts are committed, where
the founders lived, as well as revealing how their previous
associations contributed to the formation of this religion.

Many of the early roots of Mormonism were intention-
ally buried from the outset. All factions of this religion have
contributed to the falsification of its history. Therefore, anti-
Mormon writers have at times accepted the Mormon's version of their history as legitimate when it wasn't.

I have not attempted to rewrite those early years of
Mormon history. What I have attempted to do is to identify
the true source of its birth and maintain the text of that
process within the historical setting from which it emerged.
The focus then is upon the "light" of the spirit which spawned
the religion.

Joseph Smith, being the prime founder of Mormonism
and by far its most influential character, was therefore the
chief cornerstone which I felt had to be dealt with. Mormonism will stand as long as they believe he was a true prophet
of God. I know from experience that before you can totally
uproot a Mormon, he or she must question the validity of
Joseph Smith.

The book deals with several of Smith's original collabo-
rators and their perspective roles in the formation of the

Mormon conspiracy. At the same time, this book tries to place them into a setting of practical reality, where the reader will be able to simply grasp how Mormonism took root and evolved into a religion.

Very few of the lay Mormon people have ever heard of their true history, and most certainly have never caught sight of the web of deception from which Mormonism was spun.

CHAPTER ONE

The Mystery of Cumorah

❖

When I was a boy living in a Mormon community in northern Louisiana there were few places on earth where I would have rather gone than to a hill in western New York called "Hill Cumorah." Throughout the years of my childhood a deep feeling of awe and idolization developed within me as I had heard, so many times, its wondrous story of how the young Mormon prophet received from this hill golden plates from the hand of an "angel" called Moroni. A quarter of a century passed before I had the opportunity to walk upon this hill. It was a place which had become mysteriously sacred to me. That day many of the things which had been told to me as a child returned in a very vivid way. A most precious childhood dream had finally come true; I was standing where my religion was born. In my mind I could not imagine a ground more holy than the ground of Cumorah. The thrill of that day remained with me for years.

Since the year 1830 this hill, called Cumorah, has captured the affections of millions. Throughout this period of time multitudes have made their pilgrimage to this place for the purpose of basking in the wonder of its mystifying story. In their minds it easily rivals the hill where once stood the "Old Rugged Cross." I know of no other place, like Cumorah, which has been shrouded with such mystery, and where so many have believed that its "light" is the same "Light" that

came from the "Old Rugged Cross." But after the veil of
Cumorah has been lifted, and where all that was hidden is
revealed, then one beholds a "light" whose strangeness goes
far beyond what the caretakers of Cumorah's Hill are willing
to tell.

The names of these two hills tell an amazing story.
Cumorah, like Calvary, bears the mark of inspiration from
whence they sprang. The more ancient Calvary, in the Old
Testament days of the Bible, was called "Moriah," which
denotes a place of sacredness and was marked by Abraham
in prophecy where the Lamb of God would one day be slain.
Moriah would always picture in the minds of Israel a hill of
mercy, a place where God had shed His Love.

The more modern "Cumorah" suggests a connotation of
a different spirit. At first glance the name Cumorah appears
to identify with the biblical Moriah, yet a closer study reveals
that more is in its meaning than meets the eye. For *Mor-i-ah*,
removing the *i* leaves *Mor-ah*. When we study the word *Cu-
mor-ah* we learn that *Mor* means soil unsuitable for plant
growth, lacking in life giving qualities. *Ah* implies pain, sorrow, and contempt as well as an exclamation of surprise. The
portion *Cu* stands for chemical or chemic. The root *chemic*
springs out of alchemy. Alchemy means a combination of
chemistry and magic. It was a search for a process by which
cheaper metals could be turned into gold or silver.

For several years Joseph Smith, the prophet of Cumorah,
searched and dug using various forms of magic while attempting to find gold and silver in the soil of New York and
Pennsylvania. It was gold plates he claims to have found in
this very hill. The philosophical system of alchemy is a complex and mobile core of rudimentary science which is elabo-
rated with astrology, religion, mysticism, magic, theosophy,
etc. Cumorah's prophet would indeed reveal himself as an
ardent student in this field of philosophy.

In the science of the occult, word formation is very
precise and technically designed. Therefore, in the design of
the word *Cu-mor-ah* we discover a name which means "a hill
of magic where life cannot be sustained and where pain,
sorrow, contempt, and surprise is produced." Beneath those
seven letters of "Cumorah" was a prophecy of a religion that

only time could foretell. Its strange fire had long been in the minds of its "spiritual planners," as they carefully prepared the kindling for the altar they were erecting, an altar whose light was so near to the light of that "Old Rugged Cross," that only the prayerfully elect would detect the difference.

Soon the voices of this new religion would be heard singing by the anointing of that light. "The Spirit of God like a fire is burning, the latter day glory begins to come forth." And, with like fervor, "Lo, from Cumorah's lonely Hill, there comes a record of God's will. . . ."

As the flames of this religion spread, so did the love for "Cumorah's Lonely Hill." Gradually the ancient hill where once stood the Cross where Jesus was crucified drifted further and further away. This "God of Cumorah" knew there could not be two Sacred Hills. He knew eventually one would be loved and the other forgotten. This is seen in that the symbol of the Cross would be very discreetly displayed, if at all, by this religion. The preaching of the Cross has never been a popular theme among Mormon preachers.

The "Cumorah Bible" does not leave the reader with a good feeling about this hill. Rather, it leaves imbedded in his memory a picture of death without victory, pain without healing, and sorrow without joy. This book alleges two of the bloodiest battles known to man as having taken place upon this hill. Both battles were carbon copies of each other. So great was their love for the shedding of blood that both civilizations are described as fighting to the last man.

The first battle of extermination occurred some one thousand years before the second. According to the "Mormon Writing" it was about 600 B.C. when the first nation, called the Jaredites, took their blood bath. Cumorah was then called Ramah. Thus, this hill was twice bathed in blood, making it a monument unto "death." The strange accounts of this heathen massacre of two separate nations just two miles from Smith's home did not picture just the dying of men of war but also describes the awful slaughter of the women and children upon this hill.

The true nature of any religious light is always found within the makeup of its language. Cumorah, first named Ramah, is a name we read of among the pagan (demonic) religions. "Rama was aided by Hanuman, the monkey god [a demon spirit]. Rama in the Hindu religion means the sixth, seventh, and eighth incarnations of Vishnu" (re-incarnations) (Clarence Barnhart, *The World Book Dictionary*, p. 1710).

There is a hill Ramah mentioned in the Bible where the prophet Samuel was born, up in the land of rebellious Ephraim. But the real telling of Ramah was by the prophet Jeremiah where he foretold of the slaughter of the innocent: ". . . a voice was heard in Ramah, lamentation, and bitter weeping; Rachel weeping for her children refused to be comforted because they were not" (Jeremiah 31:15). Great was the weeping in America during the 1830s and 1840s, as many saw their loved ones wander off into the strange fire born of Cumorah's Hill and were blindly led from place to place.

This hill, soaked with imaginary blood as depicted in the Book of Mormon, was the womb which birthed this "alien fire" that today, together with all its factions, has become a towering inferno whose influence and powers have spread throughout the earth. Today, this religion by and far has nestled herself down into the Christian fold as one of the fair daughters of Zion. But the god who was the overseer of this "hill" in western New York has revealed a nature, both in word and in deed, far different from the God who over-saw the hill just outside of Jerusalem's gates.

The "spirit" which fathered this religion is best discerned by the name which was chosen and placed upon the book which the Mormons claim came from this hill. The choice would be unprecedented in Holy Writ. Smith was inspired to call this book, which he claimed to have received two hours past midnight on 22 September 1827, the Book of Mormon! This name carries a meaning most Mormons do not wish to discuss. From the *20th Century Webster's Unabridged Dictionary*, 1943 edition, we read that *Mormon* means, "Bugbear, something that causes needless terror by the powers of ghouls, phantoms, spirits, ghosts." In LeMoyer's *Occult 17th Century, A Treatise of Specters*, it identifies *Mormo* as a spirit in the form of a woman that terrified little children.

The selection of such a name takes on a more purposeful meaning in the light of a statement made by Willard Chase, one of Joseph's Palmyra neighbors. Willard Chase stated that Smith was required to "repair to the place where was deposited this manuscript, dressed in black clothes, and riding a black horse with a switch tail, and demand the book in a certain manner . . . They accordingly fitted out Joseph with a suit of black clothes, and borrowed a black horse." There is evidence to support Chase's claim that Smith used the color black when he went to Cumorah Hill that September night in 1827. Again folk magic suggests the reason why. Dr. Gain Robinson, "an old friend" of the Smith family, owned a store in Palmyra, and his accounting books of purchases made by the Smiths from 1825 to 1829 show that the first time any of the Smiths purchased lampblack from his store was on 18 September 1827—four days before Smith's final visit to the hill—the entry for this particular purchase beginning,

> "JOSEPH SMITH FOR" . . . Lampblack was a common pigment used to paint objects a deep black color . . . One text of ceremonial magic instructed, "neither wash yourselves at all nor dress yourselves at all in your ordinary clothes; but take a [black] Robe of Mourning . . . [on the two mornings before] familiar conversation with your Guardian Angel." and similar instructions for "a black Garment" or "robe of black" appeared several times in the 1665 edition of Scot's works and in Sibly's *Occult Sciences* upon which the Smith family's magic parchments were based . . . (D. Michael Quinn, *Early Mormonism and the Magic World View* [Salt Lake City Signature Books, Salt Lake City], 141-142)

The delusionary magic surrounding "Cumorah" is fittingly described by Brigham Young, the second Mormon prophet, who took a vast number of Smith's saints with him to the Salt Lands of Utah. He wrote the following concerning the "Mormon Hill."

> Oliver (Cowdery) says that the hill opened, and they walked into a cave, in which there was a large spacious room . . . They laid the plates on a table; and it was a large table that stood in the room. Under this table there was a pile of plates as much as two feet high, and there were altogether in this room more plates than probably

many wagon loads; they were piled up in the corners and along the walls." (*Journal of Discourses*, Vol. 19, p. 38)

This statement is an example of how "taken" the Mormon people were by the magic of Joseph Smith. The spiritist powers of Smith deceived many preachers of his day. The above account vividly illustrates the "Abracadabara" and enchanting powers which manifested in the creation of Mormonism. Lucy Mack Smith, mother of the Mormon prophet, in her book confessed their faith in the "faculty of Abraca." Mrs. Smith was also a woman adept in reading the lines of her neighbor's hands, as testified to by Mrs. Dr. Horace Mann, in *Origin of Mormonism*. Mrs. Mann was a resident of Palmyra during the time the Smith family was living there.

In an affidavit given 8 December 1833 by William Stafford, a neighbor of the Mormon prophet, we find information which is very similar to what Brigham Young had to say.

> I first became acquainted with Joseph Jr. and his family in the year 1820 . . . They would say, for instance, that in such a place, in such a hill, on a certain man's farm there were deposited kegs, barrels and hogsheads of coined silver and gold—bars of gold . . . brass kettles filled with gold and silver . . . and swords. They would say nearly all the hills in this part of New York, were thrown up by human hands, and in them were large caves, which Joseph Jr., [Mormon prophet] could see, by placing a stone of singular appearance in his hat, in such a manner as to exclude all light; at which time they pretended he could see all things within and under the earth . . . that he could see within the above mentioned caves, large gold bars and silver plates . . . that he could also discover the spirits in whose charge these treasures, were clothed in Ancient dress. (Eber D. Howe, *Mormonism Unveiled*, Painsville, Ohio, 1834, pp. 237-238)

Joseph did dig a cave some forty feet by twenty-five feet into Cumorah Hill. Several Palmyra residents were convinced some of the early writing of the Book of Mormon was performed in this cave. The entrance to the cave was shut by a metal door and was always locked. This cave was mentioned in the *Early History of Wayne County, New York* by Wayne E.

Morrison, Sr., 1969, and in *Palmyra and Vicinity* by Thomas Cook. Part of Joseph's cave, if not all of it, was the result of his digging for treasures which later developed into the "Moroni Story."

Moroni

To this day, long after the death of Joseph Smith, the spirit called "Moroni," whom Smith was to have met with on a number of occasions, continues to manifest itself among the Mormons. The following experience is further evidence that the spirit called "Moroni" is a deceiving "angel of light" which first attached itself to Joseph Smith in 1823. This spirit has not ceased its masterful art of deception among the Mormons. The following is one account among many of the manifestations of this spirit to individuals in the Mormon faith.

John H. Koyle

A resident of Spanish Fork, Utah, and very active in his duties as a leader in the local LDS Church, John H. Koyle was participant to numerous spiritual manifestations at times in his life. He had several dreams, mostly of a personal nature, which strengthened his faith and testimony of the gospel.

> Although throughout most of his life he was persecuted for his beliefs in the Nephite gold mine, he was not actually excommunicated from the Mormon Church until 1948, just a few months before his death. In fact, he served faithfully for many years as a bishop of the church in the Spanish Fork area.

> The big event took place in late August 1894, when Koyle was visited by an Angel who took him to a mountain near Salem, Utah—located south of Spanish Fork. Inside the mountain Koyle was shown an ancient Nephite gold mine filled with rich ore, gold coins and sacred records engraved on metal plates—richer than any gold mine ever to be discovered, it was to be called the Relief Mine because it would not yield its richest treasures until a time of great worldwide crisis, when all peoples and economies would need relief of an extraordinary nature.

The ancient entrances to the mine had long since caved
in, but Koyle was not to dig them out. The angel would give
directions from time to time on how to proceed. The messenger was believed to have been Moroni. (Steven Shields,
Divergent Paths of the Restoration, p. 107)

This account is but only one among thousands which
Mormons have experienced since Smith first testified of
conjuring Moroni up on that September night in 1823.

Today, standing high upon the hill which Smith named
Cumorah, is erected a statue in the honor of this spirit,
Moroni. This statue is holding in its hand a golden trumpet,
as if to be sounding the call to all the world to come and
hear its voice.

To all who desire to hear, there has been prepared an
elaborate Visitor's Center just at the base of this hill, where
they may experience the most convincing display of how
"God Almighty" incontestably revealed Himself to the world
by the means of this messenger Moroni. There within the
walls of this Center the inquirer will be privileged to hear a
very polished account of the numerous rendezvous' that
took place between Joseph Smith and the guardian spirit,
Moroni, who for centuries oversaw this ancient American
treasure. The Mormons present this spirit as an "Angel of
Heaven" coming straight from the courts of glory to an
innocent and most pure young man, whom God Himself was
to have personally visited in the year 1820.

The Mormons believe that their well-dressed fable will
be sufficient to bring their interested visitors to the knowledge of the truth. They would hope that all who come would
believe their story and search no further. But in this book
our search will go beyond the pretty words that one can hear
at the base of Cumorah Hill, down to the deepest roots,
where this *very* "Strange Religious Fire" first began to burn.

CHAPTER TWO

How the Strange Fire First Began to Burn

❖

Several years before the "Mormon fire" began to cast its first shadows upon the plains of Western New York, there were formative influences at work amidst the Green Mountains of Vermont of which the Mormons have had little to say. For several generations these influences were laying a groundwork which in time would ignite the flames of Cumorah.

> One folklorist observed that throughout the Nineteenth Century among the rural folk along the Alleghenies, particularly among the English, their Christian faith was intertwined with magic, witchcraft, sorcery, fetishism and etc., which was derived from a heathen ancestry. (J. Porter, 1894, pp. 105-106)

By the early 1800s thousands of occult books, teaching the art of that trade, were rolling off the printing presses in America. Some of the popular books were: *Book Of Knowledge* (There were thirteen American editions of this book printed in Canaan, New York.) Sibly's 1,126-page book on the occult entitled *A New and Complete Illustration of the Occult Sciences*; William Lilly wrote a book entitled *Christian Astrology*; and Hermon Kirchenhuffer's *Book of Fate* was on sale during the 1820s in Palmyra, New York, Smith's hometown. (Wayne Sentinel, 5-12-1824 and others.)

During the eighteenth century, one clergyman observed relative to the overspreading of this occult abomination, "These books and narratives are in Tradesman's Shops, and Farmer's Houses, and are read with eagerness, and are continually leavening the minds of the youth, who delight in such subjects" (Hutchinson XIV).

Historian Gordon Melton wrote that the early German immigrants to Pennsylvania "brought with them their magical faith which was seen as compatible with and supplemental to their Christian beliefs."

During his teen-age years, Joseph Smith would spend a great deal of time in Pennsylvania and the general vicinity. As we shall later see, Smith was very much at home with these people. The Whitmers (early Mormon leaders) were of German descent and were partakers of this occult heritage. John, David, and Peter Whitmer twice are noted as following the revelations produced by the "stones of crystal gazing seers" during the time they had promised their allegiance to Smith and his stone. Sometime in the year 1836, David Whitmer and a group of fellow Mormons began holding meetings at his home. The main source of attraction at this time was a young lady who began giving revelations through a "black seer stone." These meetings eventually took on a nature of secrecy and were believed to continue after David Whitmer had moved from Ohio to Missouri (Lucy Mack Smith, *Joseph Smith: The Prophet and His Progenitors*, pp. 211-212).

In and around 1800 there was a fervent religious group which formed in the state of Vermont. This group was known as the Woods' Movement. The founder was Nathaniel Woods. Many historians feel that some of Mormonism's basic spiritual "roots" were spawned from this group. These people first began their meetings and activities in Middletown, near Wells and Poultney, Vermont. They were called the "Rodsmen" due to their use of the "Witch Hazel Stick" in fortune telling, gold digging, and revelations. It was these three very things which were utilized and implemented in the early stages of the Mormon religion. The spiritual powers which controlled the Woods' Movement in Vermont seemed to intensify in manifestation among the founding fathers of Mormonism. These spirits descended in great magnitude upon Joseph Smith, Jr., its main actor, and became the main source that the early Mormons would look to for wisdom and guidance as their religion took root and began to develop.

Oliver Cowdery, one of Smith's closest associates, would be affected by the Woods' Movement. His father, William Cowdery, Jr., along with Smith's father were some of its participants. When the Smiths and Cowderys migrated to New York (Palmyra area) they brought with them this "Rodsmen Magic," as well as their beliefs in enchanted treasures. There is one thing for sure, the Smiths and Cowderys did not leave their "Green Mountain Religion" behind when they moved down to Western New York.

Most of their neighbors in Vermont would have thought it very appropriate that one of Mormonism's first revelations had to do with the "Rod." This was Joseph, Jr.'s revelation to Oliver Cowdery saying,

> Behold thou has a gift [rod], and blessed are thou because of thy gift . . . Remember it is sacred and cometh from above. And if thou wilt inquire, thou shalt know mysteries which are great and marvelous . . . Which is the gift of working with the Rod: Behold it has told you things: Behold there is no other power save God, that can cause this Rod of Nature to work in your hands . . . therefore whatsoever you shall ask me to tell you by that means, that will I grant unto you, that you shall know. (*Book of Commandments*, 7:3)

There was no "rod" in the Bible that was ever utilized to give revelations. Joseph had received this unscriptural revelation through the "seer stone" he had acquired in 1822 in Willard Chase's well.

Clark's Commentary of 1811 states that such "rods" as Cowdery had for some time been called the Rod of God, the Rod of Moses as well as the Rod of Aaron. It is interesting to note that Joseph Smith later changed the wording of this revelation to read "the Gift of Aaron" (not rod).

This practice of "rod divining" by Cowdery's, which was

condoned by Smith's revelation, is condemned in the Bible
as pure idolatry. The prophet Hosea declares, "They consult
a wooden idol and are answered by a stick of wood. A spirit
of prostitution leads them astray; they are unfaithful to their
God" (Hosea 4:12).

Quoting a Vermont publication we read,

> In the fall of 1799, some seven years before Oliver
> Cowdery was born there came to live with the Cowderys
> a Mr. Winchell (or Wingate—he had many aliases). Our
> local histories (Pemberwood family, Frisbie History of
> Middletown Springs) tells us that this man was fleeing
> from the authorities in Orange County, Vermont, where
> he was wanted for counterfeiting . . . It turned out that
> Winchell displayed unusual adeptness at the art of using
> the "hazel stick"; not for locating of underground water,
> but to find buried coins. In fact, he taught the local
> residents so well that they all took to digging for buried
> treasure, even in mid-winter.

> The Winchell matter becomes much clearer in the light
> of published evidence that Joseph Smith, Sr. was once
> implicated in counterfeiting in Orange County, Vermont,
> and that he avoided prosecution only by turning state's
> evidence. Thus, it is possible that the Smiths knew
> Winchell and that the latter was directed to the home of
> William Cowdery, Jr. (son of their old friend and neigh-
> bor in Haddam, Connecticut) by Lydia (Fuller) Gates
> Mack (Joseph Smith, Jr.'s Grandmother) (William
> Cowdery's wife, Rebecca "Fuller" was also Lydia "Fuller"
> Gates first cousin.) Once we remember the close rela-
> tionship of these people, it seems very unlikely that
> Winchell came to the Cowdery home in Wells without
> direction from someone who knew the family. (Elmer J.
> Culp, *Early Vermont Roots Of Mormonism*, Wells, Vt., pp.
> 4-5)

> Judge Frisbie, in his *History of Middletown*, writes at con-
> siderable length concerning the origin of Mormonism.
> That it took its rise in Middletown from a class of per-
> sons denominated as "rodsmen", and that one Winchell
> or Wingate, a refugee from justice in the eastern part of
> Vermont, and sought his abode in back or secluded
> places, and that he spent one winter with the same William

Cowdery ... We find that Winchell did reside with Mr.
Cowdery in the Winter of 1799 and 1800. Nancy Glass
(a cousin of Oliver Cowdery), *History of Wells, Vt.*

"I have been told that Joe Smith's father resided in
Poultney at the time of the Wood Movement here, and that
he was in it, and one of the leading rodsmen" (Hemenwaya,
1877, 3:811-812).

From the Vermont Histories we learned that Justus
Winchell fled from the authorities in Bradford, Vermont, to
William Cowdery's house in western Vermont on the other
side of the Green Mountains. One reason as to why Winchell
chose the Cowdery home stems from the old family ties
down in Connecticut, but the closeness between Smith, Sr.,
and Justus Winchell is more than happenstance. The association between Winchell and Smith becomes suspicious indeed, when we consider where Winchell was to go, who
made the arrangements for him to hide out at a Smith family
relative's home. Smith, Sr., was apparently part of the coun-
terfeiting scheme with Winchell, and to save his neck it is
possible he prepared a hiding place for Winchell at the
Cowderys while he turned states' evidence.

There is not a better place to hide than amongst old
friends and relatives. He spent the winter of 1799-1800 with
the Cowderys, concealed from the law. Shortly after Winchell
arrives in Middletown, Joseph Smith, Sr., shows up in the
same area. We know this, for his name appears on the 1800
census of Poultney, Vermont.

Justus Winchell's whole life revolved around the occult
powers of magic, and he had over the years developed close
fraternal ties with the Smith, Cowdery, Young, Lawrence,
Walter, Butt, Rockwell, Knight, Pratt families (and so forth).
From these families would come almost all of the early leaders of Mormonism. So strong were these ties that all these
families would eventually assemble together in the same
general vicinity of Palmyra, New York. This association would
extend to several other families as well. The special bond
that kept these people so close was their love and participation in the dark art of magic. It is true that some were
relatives, but it is common knowledge that believers in the
occult will always band together whenever possible.

James Lawrence and Lois Fuller (Oliver Cowdery's relative) were the parents of Samuel Lawrence. Samuel was not only a close neighbor of the Smiths down in Palmyra, but for several years was one of their close, treasure-seeking partners. The fact remains that the Lawrence, Cowdery, Walter, Beman, Rockwell, Knight, Winchell, Young (and others) all left the state of Vermont about the same time and would join with the Smiths down in Palmyra in the 1820s.

It was sometime after 1821 when the very adept Lumas (Luman) Walters moved from Vermont to Pultneyville, New York. This township was very near Sodus and put Mr. Walters only twelve to fifteen miles from where the Joseph Smith family had settled in 1816. Luman Walters, the occult professor, and Justus Winchell, the artist of the Green Mountain's Rodsmen's Magic, would quickly commence their activities shortly after moving to the general vicinity of Palmyra. Shortly after his arrival his notoriety and occult professionalism would quickly spread throughout the surrounding area of Palmyra. A family history of the Walters' family provides this information. "Family legend is that Luman Walters was a Clairvoyant" (Parfitt, 1986, p. 128).

Brigham Young, the Mormon leader who replaced Joseph Smith, described Walters as a well-traveled magician, including trips to Europe to study the sciences of the occult and the art of mesmerism. Brigham gives the following statement regarding Walters:

> I never heard such oaths fall from the lips of any man as I heard uttered by a man called the fortune teller, and who knew where the plates were (the ones Joseph claims to have found) hid. He went there three times in one summer to get them, the same summer in which Joseph did get them . . . He could tell that those plates were there, and that they were a treasure whose value to people could not be told: for that I myself heard him say. (*Journal of Discourse*, Vol. 5, p. 50)

(According to Brigham, the Mormon angel Moroni must have been sharing his secrets with more than just Joseph Smith.)

Brigham Young again states, "The man I refer to was a fortune-teller, a necromancer, and astrologer, a soothsayer, and possessed as much talent as any man that walked on the American soil, and was one of the wickedest men I ever saw . . . He would call Joseph everything bad . . . (*Journal of Discourses*, Vol. 2, pp. 180-181).

According to Brigham Young, Joseph and this fortune-teller (Lumas Walters) not only knew each other, but at times Walters became very impatient with young Smith. Brigham must have gotten his information first hand because we read in the *Palmyra Reflector* excellent verification of this.

> It is well known that Jo Smith never pretended to have any communion with angels, until a long period after the pretended finding of his book, and that the juggling of himself or father, went no further than the pretended faculty of seeing wonders in a "peep stone", and the occasional interview with the spirit, supposed to have the custody of hidden treasures; and it is also equally well known, that a vagabond fortune-teller by the name of Walters, . . . was the constant companion [sic] and bosom friend of these money digging impostors.

> There remains but little doubt, in the minds of those at all acquainted with these transactions, that Walters, who was sometimes called the conjurer, and was paid three dollars per day for his services by the money diggers in this neighborhood, first suggested to Smith the idea of finding a book. Walters, had procured an old copy of Cicero's *Orations*, in the Latin language, out of which he read long and loud to his credulous hearers, uttering at the same time an unintelligible jargon, which he would afterwards pretend to interpret, and explain, as a record of the former inhabitants of America, and a particular account of the numerous situations where they had deposited their treasures previous to their final extirpation. (*The Palmyra Reflector*, 28 February 1831)

In agreement with Brigham Young the above report testifies that Lumas Walters and Joseph Smith were constant companions and bosom friends in their activities, and that the treasures they were seeking under the guidance of their "angel spirits" were similar indeed. (Later, Joseph would marry Lumas Walters' second cousin, Emma Hale.)

To learn how deep the Smiths' occult involvement had

become would shock most any Mormon believer. Justus Winchell and Luman Walters would both have a profound influence upon the Smith family, and their development in the mysteries of the occult. In the early 1820s Walters was referred to in the Palmyra area as "Walters the Magician." Walters maintained close ties with the Smiths for two or three years in Palmyra. His influence upon Joseph, Jr., and his family was well known as being the Smiths' prime instructor into the deep secrets of necromancy, magic and divination. It was well established in the Palmyra area that "Walters the Magician" was the guide and teacher of Joseph, Jr., the Mormon prophet; and when he finally left the Smith neighborhood his "mantle" fell upon young Joseph, Jr.

By the time Walters left the neighborhood the Smith family possessed several occult lamens, talismans, special daggers for "circle drawing" and adeptness in the knowledge of occult ritualism with strong emphasis on dealing with the spells and enchantments demons held over supposed treasures. The Smith family's most intricate lamen had a central purpose that is specific in magic literature. This lamen is described in Pseudo-Aguppa's *Fourth Book of Occult Philosophy*, 1655, pp. 61-62.

According to one of Mormonism's original founding fathers, Martin Harris, Joseph Smith had been on a digging party during the evening of 22 September 1823. This is no surprise that Joseph was out trying to communicate with the treasure spirits, as this had been an on-going activity of him and his family for many years. This would be one of the charges brought out in his trial of 1826. Nevertheless, 22 September 1823 was to be the most historic night in all of Mormonism for it was on this night according to Joseph Smith that the spirit Moroni would make his first visit.

The measures that were undertaken that evening by Smith upon his return from an unsuccessful treasure capture was provided for in his family's magic parchment. There instructions were given as to how he would best proceed in order to make contact with a guardian treasure spirit. He had for several hours that same evening romanced the spirits but without success. No doubt disappointed, he turns to his family parchment in great desperation. According to Oliver Cowdery, the Mormon Church's historian in 1832, he stated that Joseph at about 11 P.M. began to make an effort to commune with some messenger. The fact that Joseph did not seek God the Father in Jesus' Name, but rather, some messenger is in itself enough evidence to see that he was seeking to make contact with someone other than the God of the Bible.

Smith had not been long in seeking for this messenger when a spirit appeared, introducing himself as Moroni. Although Smith was later to become confused over whether his name was Moroni or Nehi, most of Mormonism settled upon the name Moroni. Since this visitation or aberration is the authoritative foundation upon which the Mormon religion rests, then it is imperative that an in-depth study is made of all the surrounding circumstances of Moroni and Joseph's quest to communicate with him.

CHAPTER THREE

The "Spirit" Visitation of 1823

❖

In the early evening hours of 21 September 1823, Smith had been digging for treasures. It was about 11 P.M. that same night after arriving home that he began, according to early Mormon history, an attempt to commune with some messenger. The present Mormon history tells the story that Joseph on this evening had gone before God in great supplication in order to receive forgiveness of his sins, etc. But this story does not line up with Smith's lifestyle at that moment nor at any other point in his life thereafter. There is no evidence that Smith made any effort to surrender his life to biblical principles at that time. Rather, what we discover is that his fortune telling and "spiritist mediumship" activities with the "seer stone" continued to intensify. The pure evidence convicts Smith with the undeniable fact that he was seriously seeking the assistance of a treasure guardian demonic spirit for the purpose of ascertaining the exact location of some treasure.

To comprehend this long, drawn-out ritual of appeasement employed by Joseph Smith, Jr., on that September night in 1823 in order to secure the favoritism of the spirit-guardian whose power enchanted the treasure he was seeking, I shall quote portions of D. Michael Quinn's well-researched work on early Mormonism entitled, *Early Mormon-*

ism and Magic World View. This work was published by Signature Books of Salt Lake City, Utah. Mr. Quinn spent two years in his research through Europe, as well as in the United States, focusing primarily upon the types of magic the Smiths had utilized in their various occult ventures. All excerpts are printed by Mr. Quinn's permission.

> The Joseph Smith family possessed three magic parchments which used the names and symbols of three spirit-angels found in Scot and Sibly whose writings described these angels as appearing to men "sometimes by dreams in the night and sometimes by appearing outwardly". (Quinn, p. 115)

Martin Harris 1829 Testimony

> Perhaps even more inditing is that one of Joseph Smith's closest associates during the early days of Mormonism's formation linked the 1823 visions regarding the gold plates of the Book of Mormon with treasure seeking. This Book of Mormon witness, Martin Harris, told newspapers in 1829 that the experience was a thrice-repeated dream. He also told a Palmyra minister that these manifestations occurred after Smith had spent the earlier part of the evening acting as a seer with a group of men who were digging for treasure. (Ibid., 115)

Brigham Young

> When Brigham Young spoke "of the coming forth of the plates, from which the Book of Mormon was translated," he reverted to folk vernacular, referring to the plates five times in the next ten sentences as "that treasure" or as "the treasure", but not repeating his single reference to the gold "plates" . . . (Ibid., 116)

The reader needs to keep in mind that Brigham Young was also from the state of Vermont, and that he moved from there into the same general vicinity of Palmyra, only five to six miles from the Smiths. He apparently was part of Smith's digging party at one point in time. This is evident in that he personally knew Walters along with the other treasure seekers.

From a Spirit to an Angel

> By 1830, Smith and his followers were emphasizing that
> the messenger with whom he had dealt was an angel
> named Moroni, a soldier, prophet, and historian who
> had lived fourteen hundred years earlier on the Ameri-
> can continent. This claim caused one critic to write on
> 22 June 1830 that "Jo, made a league with the spirit, who
> afterwards turned out to be an angel" . . . Some early
> Mormons like Martin Harris continued to use both spirit
> and angel designations as late as 1831: "He told all about
> the gold plates, Angels, Spirits, and Jo Smith". (Ibid.,
> 116)

The Smith Family Laymens

Just when the Smith family had developed to this level of
occult knowledge, where they could effectively perform ritual
magic with intricately orchestrated lamens (and etc.) no one
knows, but the evidence heavily points to the years of their
close association with Luman Walters who studied, throughout Europe, the dark science of this religion. It was on this
September night that Smith was seeking to "contact some
messenger" through the medium of their family laymen.

> By all Mormon accounts, Smith met with a personage
> named Moroni who was once in possession of golden
> plates but had buried his treasure long ago to conceal it
> from those who were about to kill him . . . Such an
> account was consistent with Scot's *Discourse* on which
> one of the Smith family lamens was based . . . "Astral
> Spirits of men departed, which (if the party deceased
> was disturbed and troubled at his decease), do for many
> years, continue in the source of this world . . . When
> Treasure hath been hid, or any secret thing hath been
> committed by the party; there is a magical cause of
> something attracting the starry spirit back again, to the
> manifestation of that thing" . . . American folklore also
> described treasure-guardians, the departed spirits of
> previously murdered men who were somehow connected
> with concealed gold. (Ibid., 118-119)

Smith's Family Magical Parchment

It is very evident that Joseph was ritualistically following the occult pattern laid out in his family lamen, because the 1823 experience fits the internal dating of his family's magic parchment.

> Smith began praying late Sunday night on 21 September 1823. According to astrological guides, Sunday night was the only night of the week ruled by Jupiter ..*.. Jupiter, Smith's ruling planet, was the most prominent astrological symbol on the Smith family's golden lamen for summoning a good spirit. *Pseudo-Agrippa's Fourth Book of Occult Philosophy* also specified that "the Lord's day" was the occasion for a man "to receive an Oracle from the good spirits,' that he should place 'upon his forehead a golden lamen, upon which there must be written the name tetragrammation, as we have before spoken". . . . September 21 was also the last Sunday night in 1823 that conformed to the date references in the century).

Smith's 1823 Conjuration of a Spirit

Oliver Cowdery wrote in the 1832 *Mormon History* that Smith began praying earnestly that Sunday night about eleven or twelve in order to commune with some kind of messenger.

> The Smith family's "Jehovah, Jehovah, Jehovah" parchment specified that spirit conjurations** should begin "about eleven a clock at night," and in describing a particular conjuration "at 11 o'clock at night; not joining to himself any companion, because this particular action will admit of none . . . providing beforehand the two Seals of the Earth, drawn exactly upon parchment . . .

---

* Smith possessed a Jupiter's Talisman, see chapter 4.

** Conjuration is a process by which evil spirits are called forth to manifest with a specific purpose in mind. *The Webster's New Collegiate Dictionary* defines *conjure*, "to summons a devil or spirit by invocation or incantation." There can be no question that Smith was seeking to enlist extra–terrestrial support in his effort to locate hidden treasures that September evening in 1823 since he was continuously engaged in such efforts until the fall of 1827.

but if he desire it, they will engage to bring him the most precious [sic] of their Jewels and Riches in twenty four hours; discovering unto him the way of finding hidden treasures and the richest mines". . . . The Smith's "Holiness to the Lord" parchment has those two seals. (Ibid., 120)

A Full Moon

Smith's prayer "to commune with some kind of messenger" on 21 September 1823 occurred once the moon had reached its maximum fullness the previous day and just before the autumnal equinox . . . "And in the composition of any Circle for Magical feats, the fittest time is the brightest Moon-light". . . . An occult book published in New York in 1800 also stated, "Dreams are most to be depended on by men at the full of the moon". . . . Because the full moon was the preferred time for treasure digging, it is probably no coincidence that, according to Martin Harris, Smith acted as treasure-seer earlier that night. . . . In fact, his prayer 'to commune with some kind of messenger' may have been in response to an unsuccessful group effort earlier that evening to locate a treasure in the hill. (Ibid., 120-121)

Midnight Ideal for Communion

Like previous occult guides . . . specified in a chart of "Angels and Planets ruling SUNDAY," that for the twelfth hour of the night (eleven to midnight), the rulers were Mercury and Raphael. . . . Therefore, the hour and day in which Smith prayed "to commune with some kind of messenger" was pinpointed in magic books as being ideal for the invocation of spirits. Also, the angel of that hour, Raphael, figured prominently at the center of the Smith family's most significant lamen . . . which was constructed to aid a treasure quest. . . . The appearance of treasure spirits at 11 P.M., the hour before midnight, continued in popular folklore through the mid-nineteenth century. . . .

Even the time at which Joseph Smith said the communication ended echoed the requirements of magic invocation. Joseph Smith said the messenger ascended just

before sunrise . . . and *Pseudo-Agrippa's Fourth Book of
Occult Philosophy* specified that spirit conjuration must
conclude "before the rising of the sun". (Ibid., 121)

The Mormon Hill

All Mormon accounts agree that sometime during the
daylight hours of Monday morning, Joseph Smith went
to the nearby hill . . . in Manchester,* where he discovered the gold plates of the Book of Mormon. A resident
of Manchester later wrote, "Mormon Hill" had long been
designated "as the place in which countless treasures
were buried"; Joseph the elder, had "spaded" up many
a foot of the hill side to find them, and Joseph Jr. had
on more than one occasion accompanied him". . . . Both
Mormon and non-Mormon sources agree that Joseph
Smith used his brown treasure-seeking stone to discover
the gold plates on this occasion. (Emphasis added. Ibid.,
122)

Plates Discovered by Magical Means

Although much has been said about Smith finding gold
plates in the "Hill" near his home, there exists no historical
validation of him ever truly finding any plates at all. What
does exist is an account of Smith utilizing the powers of
magic to convince the unwary to testify of their reality.

In 1833, one Palmyra resident testified that Smith told
him "he looked in his stone and saw them in the place
of deposit". . . . while Willard Chase stated that Smith
told him in the fall of 1827 that without the stone he
found in the Chase well "he would not have obtained the
book. . . ."

And if there were any doubt about the matter, early
Mormon Hosea Stout recorded in February 1856 that
"President [Brigham] Young exhibited the Seer's stone
with which The Prophet Joseph discovered the plates of
the Book of Mormon, to the Regents [of the University
of Deseret Utah] this evening. It is said to be a siliceous
granite dark color almost black with light colored stripes."
(Ibid., 122)

---

*Manchester is a town 4 miles south of Palmyra.

When Smith Finds the Plates

The earliest available Mormon history of Smith's next experience, during the day of 22 September 1823, was dictated by Smith in 1832: "Then I immediately went to the place and found where the plates was deposited as the angel of the Lord had commanded me and straightway made three attempts to get them. Then being exceedingly frightened I supposed it had been a dream of Vision" . . . This account as later revised by Smith in 1838 and officially published in 1842 omits four important details from the above: the three unsuccessful attempts, Smith's fear, his failure to keep a certain commandment, and his desire to obtain riches by visiting the hill Cumorah. (Ibid., 123)

(These four details were attested to by Smith's neighbors in their testimonies, but would be accused by Mormon apologists of having exaggerated the facts.)

Source of Smith's Fear

Other early sources affirm these details of Smith's 1832 narrative. The 1833 affidavit of Palmyra resident Willard Chase, which contains more parallels to Mormon sources than any other affidavit . . . refers specifically to "his fright," the three attempts, and the rebuke for not having "obeyed your orders," although Chase does not specify what those orders were and makes no reference to the desire for riches. . . .

Traditional Mormon sources, including all of Smith's autobiographies from 1832 on, are silent about the specific cause of Smith's fear or as to why he would be astonished at the appearance of Moroni on the hill. One non-Mormon source provides a possible answer, however. Willard Chase's 1833 affidavit specifically identified the source of that fear: "He saw in the box something like a toad, which soon assumed the appearance of a man, and struck him on the side of his head." E. D. Howe, who published Chase's testimony in *Mormonism Unveiled*, restated Chase's testimony to read: "looked into the hole, where he saw a toad, which immediately transformed itself into a spirit." (Ibid., 123-124)

Benjamin Saunders

It would be difficult to find a source more friendly to
Smith in Palmyra. This is what Benjamin Saunders had
to say about the coming forth of the Book of Mormon:
"I heard Joe tell my Mother and Sister how he procured
the plates. He said he was directed by an angel where it
was. He went in the night to get the plates. When he
took the plates there was something down near the box
that looked some like a toad that rose up into a man
which forbid him to take the plates. . . . He told his story
just as earnestly as any one could. (Ibid., 126)

The Toad

In the Anglo-American occult tradition, if not generally,
the toad has always been associated with Satanism, black
magic, sorcery, and witchcraft. . . . Thus, if a toad were
a treasure-guardian, as Howe was suggesting, it would
necessarily be "a devil, in the shape of a gigantic toad".
. . . The only other amphibian which, according to the
magic world view, could appear in human or spirit form
is the salamander. (Ibid., 128)

The Fiery Salamander

The belief that fiery salamander spirits could communicate with humans is at least as old as the Middle Ages. . . ."
The most detailed story of salamander communication is E.
T. W. Hoffmann's tale, *The Golden Pot*. First published as one
of his *Fantasiestuecke* in 1814, it went through three editions
from 1814 to 1825, and Thomas Carlyle translated it into
English in 1827. In this short story, a mysterious record-
keeper, "sprung from the wondrous race of the Salamanders
(Ibid., 130-131).

Spirits Commission a Young Man

Spirits of the "Elements," commissions a young man to
transcribe "a number of manuscripts, partly Arabic,
Coptic, and some of them in strange characters, which
belong not to any known tongue." The salamander archivist, who appears outwardly as a man, has preserved

these characters through the years. The story includes an incantation at eleven P.M. on the September equinox, the use of a stone for revelations, and a dramatic scene in which the salamander archivist uses his powers to conquer "Satanic arts". . . . Paracelsus had earlier written that fiery salamander spirits were guardians for "hidden treasures that must not be revealed yet." (Ibid, p. 131)

The account was duplicated exactly by Smith in every detail. Smith had been using his stone for years in attempting to conquer Satanic Arts.

The Salamander Moroni

If Smith saw a salamander on the hill, rather than a toad, this would have been consistent with magic associations concerning the name Moroni and occult traditions concerning the salamander. For early nineteenth-century Americans, the spirit messenger's name Moroni could have evoked "moron," an American Indian word for an agent of poison; "Moron," a name of magic invocation; "Moron," the scientific term for a poisonous salamander; as well as the elemental spirit of fire in traditional magic lore. (Ibid., 132)

Setnau and His Gold Box

Finally, the salamander version of the coming forth of the Book of Mormon also has archetypal parallels. So far as is known, the fourth century B.C. "Story of Setnau" was not translated from Egyptian into a European language until 1867. In this story, Setnau is directed to find a book of magic in a gold box, contained in successively larger boxes of declining preciousness. As a parallel to the three Moroni visits in 1823, Setnau takes three days and nights to discover the gold box after receiving instructions about its location. (Ibid., 133)

The evidence is very conclusive that Moroni was a spirit demon conjured up by Joseph Smith in the late hours of the 22d day of September, 1823. In his mother's writings she agrees with the neighbors that Joseph was knocked down three times when attempting to get the plates. Smith himself agreed that he made three unsuccessful attempts.

It is a well-known fact among deliverance ministers that demons seize every opportunity to inflict pain upon a person, as well as to manifest in various shapes and forms. According to the Smith family and his neighbors Joseph had told of a very bizarre happening having occurred out there on Cumorah's Hill. It was such a frightful ordeal for the twenty-two-year-old rising prophet that he is found still speaking of how frightened he was, as he and Cowdery were writing the 1834 *History of Mormonism* some seven years later. Smith's own words were, "being exceedingly frightened." This spirit did not respond, according to the normal scriptural pattern, as established by the angels of Heaven. Their response would have been, "fear not, be not afraid." They would not knock the "Lord's Anointed" down three times, and scare him out of his wits.

Whether Moroni chose to become a toad or a salamander seemed to have made little difference to Joseph. His heart was set on retrieving the treasure regardless of the cost. Every year on 22 September from 1823 on, Joseph was to meet with this spirit until every detail of obedience had been fulfilled by him. First, Joseph was told to bring his older brother, Alvin, and that would appease the spirit for the treasure's release, but Alvin died before the appointed time. Sometimes the spirits will accept portions of a dead man's body; thus a story arose there in Palmyra that Alvin's body had been dug up for this cause. To quell the widespread rumor, Smith, Sr., ran a statement in the local paper for several weeks, denying it all. One day Joseph took his old friend Samuel Lawrence out to Cumorah in hopes that the spirit would approve, but to no avail.

According to one of Smith's neighbors, Joseph had confided in him that the spirit was willing to accept as a substitute for Alvin the daughter of Isaac Hale whom Joseph was acquainted with. Just how Smith importuned the spirit Moroni to accept her is not clear. Nevertheless, Lucy Smith, Joseph's mother, in her book about Joseph, goes into some detail to describe Joseph's breaking with family tradition and marrying several years before the accepted age.

The securing of Emma Hale was so important to Smith that he somehow arranged for her to visit some mutual friends, and there he would meet her. Together with the help of his friend and no doubt his spirit guide, Moroni, they persuaded Emma to marry Joseph immediately. So urgent was the matter that Emma's opportunity for a wedding like most normal girls was snatched from her by the "bewitchment" of her husband to be. And as history records it, on 18 January 1827 the marriage took place in South Bainbridge, New York, unbeknown to Emma Hale's parents. (One account has Oliver Cowdery as Joseph's best man.)

If Emma would go with Smith to the hill perhaps he could now fulfill the spirit's command, and if there were no more "salamandering surprises," just maybe this over demanding, cruel, demonic Moroni may allow Smith to realize his desires. Apparently this spirit still wasn't going to be easy on Smith, for the word was communicated to him either via his "Seer Stone" or by a toad that he was to repair to Cumorah at 2 A.M. on 22 September 1827, to obtain the treasure.

The story now changes among Smith's neighbors; the news which Smith now relates is that the treasure is a stack of gold plates upon which is written the ancient history of the American Indian. Everyone wants to see Smith's find, even his weary old parents, who suffered through all of Moroni's harassments of their son, his own brothers and sisters, and his wife, Emma, who sacrificed the wishes of her family. But all are denied even a single peek at the "Treasure of the Toad." To even glance, Smith warned, would be instant death. The "Curse of Death" was placed upon what the Mormons testify as being a record containing the "Word of God."

Smith, in the years that followed, would not hesitate to utilize the power of a curse in any situation which would assist him to accomplish his own desires. Smith had learned the art of deception extremely well and no one was going to "teeter" him from its pathway.

CHAPTER FOUR

From Water Witching to Talismanic Power

❖

In 1829 Jesse Smith, the uncle of Joseph and Hyrum Smith, wrote a letter of warning to Hyrum. It was advising Hyrum about their belief and participation in magic. This letter (Quinn, *Mormonism*, p. 28-29) expresses their uncle's deep concern over the spiritual welfare of his relatives. It also revealed that he was fully aware of their involvement in the occult. Thus, he warned Hyrum of the evil of their practice and told him that Jannes and Jambres, who withstood Moses in Egypt, had operated under the same demonic power in which they were all involved.

The failure of Joseph to give heed to his Uncle Jesse's letter reveals that the young Mormon seer was not only in deep league with the powers which possessed him, but it also reveals that he did not understand the Christian standard which separated a true prophet of God from a false one. Pride and blindness of heart will cause a man to do many vain and foolish things. One such foolishness is to ignore sound scriptural counsel when God sends it to a man, regardless of whether it is from your own uncle.

Smith's experimental knowledge as a prophet is seen in the teaching where he taught his followers that the way to discern true angels from false angels was by the color of their hair (Joseph Smith, *Times and Seasons*, 1 April 1842, vol. 3, p. 747).

But in the final analysis, Joseph Smith was a false prophet because he chose to put his word above the written Word of God. It was early on in his life when he yielded himself to various spirits of darkness, from which he was never freed. These spirits drove Smith to fame, fortune, power, polygamy, and on into a proclamation that Lucifer was the true light; that he, Joseph, was a god; and that all men can become gods.

Finally, these spirits drove Joseph Smith to an early grave. The Bible tells us, "The thief cometh not, but for to steal, and to kill, and to destroy . . . " (John 10:10). One year before his death in Carthage, Illinois, Joseph prophesied to his followers in Nauvoo that no man could take his life for the next five years (letter written by Sarah Scott, 22 July 1844, Nauvoo, Illinois).

The Bible states that the wheels of God grind slowly, but they grind exceedingly finely. The divine wheel of judgment finally caught up with Smith in Carthage, Illinois, in the year 1844. His high-rolling life of deception, as well as his abuse of the social and political system was permitted to go no further. This "tragedy" had its beginning in disobedience—a disobedience which originated from a disrespect to the following of the Word of God,

> There shall not be found among you any one that maketh his son or his daughter to pass through the fire, or that useth divination, or an observer of times, or an enchanter, or a witch. Or a charmer, or a consulter with familiar spirits, or a wizard, or a necromancer. For all . that do these things are an abomination unto the Lord: and because of these abominations the Lord thy God doth drive them out from before thee. (Deut. 18:110-112)

Perhaps the saga of Joseph Smith would have ended far differently had he been given the proper scriptural instruction by his parents. If he had been given sound Bible teaching, he would have known then that the occult was forbidden ground. One Palmyra resident who knew the Smiths described Joseph's father: "This Joseph Smith Senior, we soon learned from his own lips, was a firm believer in witchcraft and other supernatural things; and had brought up his family in the same belief" (Lapham, 1870, 2:384; D. Morgan, 1986, 220-221).

One of Joseph's close neighbors describes an experience in Smith's young life, which may have been the turning point that set the course which led to that pitiful day in Carthage.

> I became acquainted with the Smith family . . . in the year 1820. At that time, they were engaged in the money digging business, which they followed until the later part of the season of 1827. In the year 1822, I was engaged in digging a well. I employed Alvin and Joseph Smith to assist me . . . After digging about twenty feet below the surface of the earth, we discovered a singularly appearing stone, which excited my curiosity. I brought it to the top of the well, and as we were examining it, Joseph put it into his hat, and then his face into the top of his hat . . . The, next morning he came to me, and wished to obtain the stone, alleging that he could see in it ... . He (Joseph Smith) then observed that if it had not been for that stone (which he acknowledged belonged to me), he would not have obtained the book. . . . (Eber D. Howe, *Mormonism Unveiled*, Painesville, Ohio, 1834, pp. 240–242, 246, 247)

Joseph was probably over at Mr. Chase's that day because of his water witching ability (working of the rod), to help Mr. Chase ascertain where the water might be found. Water witching has been innocently, as well as ignorantly, believed in for centuries.

Several years ago, when I was a boy of about nine years of age, my grandfather came over to my house to help my dad locate the best spot to dig a well. I remember walking out to a peach tree with my grandfather as he took his knife and cut a forked limb from the tree. I remember asking him, "Why a peach tree limb?" He said, "They work better." I watched as he walked about the yard and observed for some time how that stick would move, quiver, and bend. I saw it go from a straight-out position and do a curved nose dive toward the ground. This was "strange stuff" to a nine-year-old. I was impressed with my grandfather's ability to determine where the underground water stream was.

I readily embraced the deception believed by my grandfather and father. I was convinced that day that the underground water was the "cause" of the erratic movements of
the "peach stick." Then, my grandfather spoke, "Connie,
[speaking to my dad] the spot for the well is right here." The
stick was in a quivering nose dive next to the ground. "I'll
prove it to you," he said. He turned around and proceeded
to walk directly away with his back to the spot with the
"divining rod" pointing out in front of him. When he had
taken about three steps the "divining rod" began to lift
upward; with my grandfather holding it firmly, it continued
to bow up and back toward the "spot." As it quivered up
toward my grandfather's face both branches of this "divining
rod" instantly snapped in two at the edge of my grandfather's
hands. I stood with eyes of disbelief. Never had I witnessed
a stick to curve upward, quiver, and then snap in two all by
itself! It would be several years later before I was to learn
whose power was operating in the "water ritual" that day.

Perhaps a good name for the "stone" that Smith found
that day at the home of Willard Chase would be the "Chase
Stone," because, the chase would soon be on. Joseph would
be chased from Palmyra, mostly in fear of being exposed; on
to Kirtland, where he would, before the face of his own
converts, be chased out of Kirtland to the frontier of Missouri. From there he would be chased into western Illinois,
with the chase continuing even after his death as his followers scattered to the four winds—some fleeing to Texas, Michi-
gan, Pennsylvania, and to the Rocky Mountains; even to a
salt land uninhabited (Jeremiah 17:6).

Only works of darkness can spread such paths of foolishness, heartbreak, suffering, and sorrows. All because one
man found a "stone" twenty-three feet down in a well and
thought he had found the pearl of great price. He certainly
esteemed the "stone" precious above all others. After refus-
ing to return the stone to Mr. Chase (a form of stealing), his
notoriety of having special divining powers began to spread
rapidly throughout the surrounding counties. Soon, by 1824,
Joseph's reputation as a "seer" had spread over one hundred
miles away. From that distance arrived a man by the name

of Josiah Stowell, who traveled from Chenanago County, New York, to Palmyra to look up Joseph. Lucy Smith writes, "He came for Joseph on account of having heard that he possessed certain keys, by which he could discern things invisible to the natural eye" (Lucy Mack Smith, *Joseph Smith: The Prophet and His Progenitors*, p. 91-92).

Joseph and several others decided to go with Stowell where Joseph would utilize his special keys of discernment in locating the enchanted Spanish Treasures. The others would do the digging while Smith would direct the operation by special revelations as they were given to him through his "seer stone." However, this was not to be a pleasant trip for Smith. He was to get into serious trouble while working for Mr. Stowell. There, in southern New York, he would be arrested as a disorderly person and brought to trial 20 March 1826 at Bainbridge, New York. A portion of that record is as follows:

> State of New York vs. Joseph Smith
>
> Warrant issued upon written complaint upon the oath of Peter G. Bridgeman, who informed that one Joseph Smith of Bainbridge was a disorderly person and an imposter. "Prisoner brought before Court March 20, 1826. Prisoner examined: says this: he came from the town of Palmyra, and had been at the house of Josiah Stowell in Bainbridge . . . That he had a certain 'stone' which he had occasionally looked at to determine where hidden treasures in the bowels of the earth were. He professed to tell in this manner where gold mines were a distance under the ground, and had looked for Mr. Stowell several times, and had informed him where he could find these treasures . . . That at Palmyra he pretended to tell by looking at this stone where coin money was buried in Pennsylvania, and while at Palmyra had frequently ascertained in that way where lost property was of various kinds. . . ." (*Frazier Magazine*, February 1873, p. 229) Justice Albert Neely presided.

Smith was found guilty of the charges and was fined. The court bill read, "Joseph Smith the Glasslooker." Joseph Smith and all Mormons have denied that such a record had ever existed. But, thanks to Wesley Walters, it was rediscovered in 1971.

Deception by occult powers is very much the same as being in bondage to drugs or alcohol. Being arrested, tried, and found guilty does not always affect a change. Often plans of the next venture are already in the making, even before the courtroom door closes. It was that way with Smith; the addiction with the spirit was too strong, he could not lay the "stone" down and walk away. The reason he would not lay down these "certain keys" which his mother said he possessed was because, for the past five or more years, his fellowship with these spirits of divination had continued to intensify. They had become his constant companions and were the source of his prophetic anointing. Smith therefore had no plans of bidding them to go.

He may not have realized in 1826 the actual depth of deception and ruinations these spirits would eventually take him. He seemed undaunted by the trial. His problems with the "law" would become a yearly ordeal and would eventually consummate eighteen years later in a jailhouse in Carthage, Illinois.

There were several witnesses in this 1826 trial, one of which was a Mr. Thompson, an employer of Mr. Stowell. The following scene was described by this witness, and carefully noted:

> Smith had told the Deacon that several years before, a band of robbers had buried on his flat a box of treasure, and as it was very valuable they had, by a sacrifice, placed a charm over it to protect it, so that it could not be obtained except by faith, accompanied by certain talismatic influences. So, after arming themselves with fasting and prayer, they sallied forth to the spot designated by Smith. Digging was commenced with fear and trembling, in the presence of this imaginary charm. In a few feet from the surface the box of treasure was struck by the shovel, on which they redoubled their energies, but it gradually receded from their grasp. One of the men placed his hand upon the box, but it gradually sunk from his reach. . . . Mr. Stowell went to his flock and selected a fine vigorous lamb, and resolved to sacrifice it to the demon spirit who guarded the coveted treasure.

> Shortly after the venerable Deacon might be seen on his
> knees at prayer near the pit, while Smith, with a lantern
> in one hand to dispel the midnight darkness might be
> seen making a circuit around the spot, sprinkling the
> flowing blood from the lamb upon the ground, as a
> propitiation to the spirit that thwarted them. They then
> descended the excavation, but the treasure still receded
> from their grasp, and it was never obtained . . . (Gerald
> Tanner, *Mormonism Shadow or Reality*, p. 37)

According to the above testimony of Mr. Thompson,
Smith told him that it would take "faith" to get the box. This
would be the same requirement that Joseph would later use
on those that desired to be witnesses of the Book of Mormon. The soothsayer will tell you that mental faith is an
important principle which must operate before there can be
any success in the occult world. In this testimony Joseph puts
forth some astounding occult knowledge for a youngster of
twenty or twenty-one. The "box" could not be obtained except by "faith," accompanied by certain talismanic influences.
How could Joseph understand the "spirit powers" of a talisman, unless, by extensive in-depth instruction? For a young
man to understand the principles of "faith" and talismanic
influences, and how these are to be simultaneously employed
into one function, so as to secure the release of sought-after
treasures from the enchanting powers, is truly amazing for
a young Mormon prophet in the making.

In 1974 a Mormon professor delivered a lecture concerning the talisman that Joseph Smith owned. It could have
been the same talisman he was using in 1826. The following
is a portion of a presentation made by Dr. Reed Durham,
LDS Institute of Religion director, to a Mormon History
Association 20 April 1974:

> . . . I should like to initiate all of you into what is perhaps
> the strangest, the most mysterious, occult-like esoteric,
> and yet Masonically oriented practice ever adopted by
> Joseph Smith. . . . All available evidence suggests that
> Joseph Smith the Prophet possessed a magical Masonic
> medallion, or talisman, which he worked during his life-
> time and which was evidently on his person when he was
> martyred. His talisman is in the shape of a silver dollar
> and is probably made of silver or tin. It is exactly one

and nine-sixteenths inches in diameter, . . . the talisman, . . . originally purchased from the Emma Smith
Bidamon family, fully notarized by that family to be
authentic and to have belonged to Joseph Smith, can
now be identified as a Jupiter talisman . . . I wasn't able
to find what this was, for—as I said—two months; and
finally, in a magic book printed in England in 1801,
published in America in 1804, and I traced it to Manchester, and to New York.

It was a magic book by Francis Barrett and, lo and
behold, how thrilled I was when I saw in his list of magic
seals the very talisman which Joseph Smith had in his
possession at the time of his martyrdom . . . To the Egyp-
tians, Jupiter was known as Ammon, but to the Greeks
he was Zeus: the ancient sky Father, or Father of the
Gods. . . .

In astrology, Jupiter is always associated with high positions, getting one's own way, and all forms of status.
And I quote: "Typically a person born under Jupiter will
have the dignity of a natural ruler. . . . He will probably
have an impressive manner. . . . In physical appearance,
the highly developed Jupiterian is strong, personable,
and often handsome. . . . the Jupiterian influence produces a cheerful winning personality, capable of great
development". . . . (A word on magic: "a person skilled
in sorcery; any occult art or science, especially the supposed art of putting in action the power of spirits. The
science of producing wonderful effects by the aid of
superhuman beings. An expressed agreement between
humans and demons.")

So closely is magic bound up with the stars and astrology
that the term astrologer and magician were in ancient
times almost synonymous. The purpose of the Table of
Jupiter in talismatic magis [magic?] was to be able to call
upon the celestial intelligences, assigned to the particular talisman, to assist one in all endeavors. The names of
the deities which we gave to you who could be invoked
by the Table were always written on the talisman or
represented by various numbers. Three such names were
written on Joseph Smith's talisman: Abbah, Father; El
Ob, Father is God or God the Father; and Josiphiel;
Jehovah speaks for God, the Intelligence of Jupiter.

When properly invoked, with Jupiter being very powerful and ruling in the heavens, these intelligences—by the power of ancient magic—guaranteed to the possessor of this talisman the gain of riches, and favor, and power, and love and peace; and to confirm honors, and dignities, and councils. Talismatic magic further declared that any one who worked skillfully with this Jupiter Table would obtain the power of stimulating anyone to offer his love to the possessor of the talisman, whether from a friend, brother, relative, or even any female (David C. Martin, *Mormon Miscellaneous*, Vol. 1, No. 1, October 1975, pp. 14-15). The above information has to raise the question of just how deep was Smith in league with these dark powers?

Returning to the trial of 1826, we find that a Jupiter (God) talisman apparently was in his possession at the time of his arrest, because Smith claimed that the treasure could only be obtained by talismanic influences. He certainly would not have traveled 100 miles to obtain a treasure from the earth which was held fast by a power of enchantment without the proper equipment necessary to break through the "spell" of these spirits.

Mr. Durham stated in the paragraph above that Joseph's talisman, when skillfully attended to, would stimulate male or female to offer his or her love to the possessor.

Joseph's talismanic power can be seen affecting such a stimulation in the lives of both Oliver Cowdery and Lucy Walker. Cowdery states the following in paragraph three of his *Defence*,

> There was a time when I thought myself able to prove to the satisfaction of every man that the translator of the Book of Mormon, was worthy of the appellation of a Seer and a Prophet of the Lord, and in which he held over me a mysterious power which even now I fail to fathom; but I fear I may have been deceived, and especially so fear since knowing that Satan has led his mind astray.

Cowdery knew of Smith's "seer stone" but apparently was not fully appraised of Joseph's talismanic powers.

In Fawn Brodie's book, *No Man Knows My History*, on

pages 337 and 338 we read of Joseph's power of subjugation
over those near him:

> Six of the girls Joseph took as wives lived at various times
> as wards in his own home. These were the Partridge
> sisters, the Lawrence sisters, Eliza R. Snow, and Lucy
> Walker. One of these, the seventeen-year-old Lucy Walker,
> who had moved into the prophet's home after the death
> of her mother, described Joseph's whirlwind courtship.
> She thereby revealed not only her own ingenuousness
> but also Joseph's sophistication. Late in April, 1843,
> Emma Smith went to St. Louis to make purchases for
> the Mansion House, accompanied by Lucy's brother,
> Lorin Walker, who was one of Joseph's business aides.
> During their absence Joseph asked Lucy to become his
> wife.

> "I have no flattering words to offer," he told her after
> the usual preliminaries. "It is a command of God to you.
> I will give you until tomorrow to decide this matter. If
> you reject this message the gate will be closed forever
> against you."

> "This," she said, "aroused every drop of Scotch in my
> veins. For a few moments I stood fearless before him,
> and looked him in the eye. I felt at this moment that I
> was called to place myself upon the altar a living sacri-
> fice—perhaps to brook the world in disgrace and incur
> the displeasure and contempt of my youthful compan-
> ions."

> "Although you are a Prophet of God," she told him,
> "you could not induce me to take a step of so great
> importance, unless I knew that God approved my course.
> I would rather die."

> He walked across the room, returned, and stood before
> her with what she described as "the most beautiful ex-
> pression of countenance," and said: "God Almighty bless
> you. You shall have a manifestation of the will of God
> concerning you; a testimony that you can never deny. I
> will tell you what it shall be. It shall be that joy and peace
> that you never knew."

> "Oh how earnestly I prayed for these words to be ful-
> filled," Lucy said. "It was near dawn after another sleep-

less night when my room was lighted up by a heavenly influence. To me it was, in comparison, like the brilliant sun bursting through the darkest cloud. My soul was filled with a calm, sweet peace that 'I never knew.' Supreme happiness took possession of me, and I received a powerful and irresistible testimony of the truth of plural marriage."

In the early Mormon Church no person close to Joseph Smith was exempt from the powerful spirit influences of control and persuasion. There were hundreds, if not thousands, who were mesmerized by these powers as they became his slaves, while thinking they were faithfully carrying out the will of God.

CHAPTER FIVE

The Smiths and the Unity Preacher

❖

Lucy Mack Smith, the mother of the Mormon prophet, writes, "Shortly after the death of Alvin (her oldest son), a man commenced laboring in the neighborhood, to effect a union of the different churches, in order that all might be agreed, and thus worship God with one heart and with one mind" (Lucy Mack Smith, *Joseph Smith: The Prophet and His Progenitors*, 1853 Edition, p. 90).

Since Alvin died in November of 1824, this preacher of unity would have visited Palmyra sometime between 1825 to 1827 to hold his meetings. Lucy wrote her family memoirs in 1853. Since Alvin's death would have become a major point in her chronology, an event occurring twenty-four months after his death would certainly be considered "shortly after." A look into the visit of the "Unity Preacher" is crucial, since it was a preacher of that same faith that would very shortly thereafter come to play a major role in the rise of Mormonism.

Stanley Stuber, author of *Where We Got Our Denominations*, on pages 224-229, helps us to understand the "Unity Preachers" of that day. Speaking of the Disciple of Christ Church, he heads his chapter, "The Church of Unity."

During the revival movements in the early part of the nineteenth century there arose a people who stood for

59

the Bible alone without the aid of creeds and formulas.
Thomas Campbell . . . and his son, Alexander Campbell,
formed an organization called the "Christian Association of Washington, Pennsylvania." However it was not
the wish of these leaders that this association might
become a distinct denomination . . . believers in restoration rather than in reformation . . . to restore primitive
Christianity, with all beliefs and practices. . . . They
purposed to return to the pattern of the first church, as
found in the New Testament. . . . The Disciples called
themselves a "peculiar people." This does not mean that
they considered themselves odd or as standing off from
others, but because they yearned for unity and for full
Christian fellowship. They not only believed in unity;
they claimed to have found the path to unity in restoration of simple New Testament Christianity.

The description of the Unity Preacher given by Lucy
Smith in our first paragraph is in complete harmony with
the Campbellite definition given by Stuber in the above.
There is no other conclusion to be drawn regarding the
Unity Preacher than that he was a Disciple of Christ. Joseph's
mother further remarks on pages 91 and 92 of her book,
"To gratify me, my husband attended some two or three
meetings. . . . During this excitement Joseph would say, it
would do us no injury to join them."

Joseph Smith left home for Pennsylvania in the fall of
1825 and did not return until late spring in 1826. But Lucy
gives conclusive evidence that Joseph was at home at the
time the Unity Preacher was there. Therefore, the time of
the Unity Preacher's visit to Palmyra could have been as late
as the spring of 1827. Lorenzo Saunders, a neighbor of the
Smiths, claims that a Unity Preacher by the name of Sidney
Rigdon was seen at that same time in Palmyra visiting the
Smiths.

Therefore, Rigdon must have been the preacher of which
Lucy was identifying in her family history. In her older years
she would have been very appreciative of the help which
Rigdon had given to her son, Joseph, in the formation of the
Mormon Church. For Lucy Mack to give so much attention
to these "Disciples of Christ" meetings there in their neighborhood is both suspicious and enlightening. Why would

she ramble on about this one event, and make such a big deal out of it, except that in her efforts she is trying to give Sidney Rigdon some place in her family's personal history during that period of time, without revealing his name.

I remember when I was a boy and preachers came into the neighborhood. The neighbors would make their plans, so that the preacher would eat fried chicken at our house one day, and the next day at the neighbors, until all who wished could have the preacher bless their home with his presence. Now, Lucy and her family thought highly of this preacher man and apparently she was well taken by his preaching. It would be difficult to try to imagine that Lucy would allow such a wonderful occasion to pass by and not have this preacher taste her cooking. I suspect this "man of the cloth" more than once put his feet under her table. As she said on page 90 of her book, "this seemed about right to me and I felt much inclined to join in with them."

Now, from all the above we are learning that Joseph Smith did in all probability meet a "Disciple of Christ" minister sometime after the death of his brother, Alvin, in November 1824. But Joseph's mother, Lucy, for some unknown reason absolutely refused to divulge the preacher's name, when on other occasions she could remember names of persons she had met only one time.

The history records tell us that in July of 1821, Adamson Bently (Rigdon's brother-in-law by marriage) and Sidney Rigdon visited Alexander Campbell, one of the founders of the Disciples of Christ, to discuss joining the Disciple work. This was agreed upon and in February 1822, Rigdon accepted a (Baptist) Church in Pittsburgh, Pennsylvania, with help from Alexander Campbell. On the following 11 October 1823, he was released because of preaching certain doctrines which the Baptists could not accept. Therefore, with further assistance from Campbell and Scott, Rigdon moved more fully into the Disciple's ministry of the "union gospel."

With some certainty that Sidney Rigdon was the Disciple Unity preacher that Joseph's mother was writing about, and that he and young Smith had the opportunity to engage in a conversation, and knowing what we do, perhaps we could in some semblance reconstruct some of that conversation. When considering Joseph's extensive treasure hunting activities among the mounds of western New York and the caves of Pennsylvania, he would have wanted to know what Rigdon knew about the Ohio Mounds and the aborigines in that part of the country.

According to his mother, Lucy, Joseph had already been fantasizing over these original inhabitants of America. For in her book we read, "He would describe the ancient inhabitants of this continent, their dress, mode of travelling, and the animals upon which they rode (Joseph wrote 'horses' in the Book of Mormon, but, the Spaniards brought horses over with them); their cities, their buildings, with every particular; their modes of warfare; and also their religious worship. This he would do with as much ease, seemingly, as if he had spent his whole life with them" (Lucy Mack Smith, *Joseph Smith: The Prophet and His Progenitors*, 1853 edition, p. 85). This statement could possibly contain a little of "mother's exaggeration."

Joseph most likely would have told Rigdon of all his endeavors to find ancient hidden treasures, as well as his hope to discover some clue to the riddle about the aborigines. There were during this period of history many voices floating all over the Western Reserve, speculating concerning the origin of these aborigines.

Rigdon on the other hand, living on the frontier, could easily identify with Smith's curiosity and to some extent his digging for the hidden treasures (Rigdon would in 1836 go on a treasure hunt with Smith.). Sidney would have listened to the talkative young man in great interest, and then at the most timely place give some purposeful guidance to the conversations such as, "Joseph, would it not be beyond the possibility that a record, perhaps a book, could lay hidden just beneath the surface waiting to be found."

"It is interesting Brother Rigdon that you bring that up; I have recently seen such things through my 'seer stone,' that some treasure of that sort does exist. One of my good friends, Luman Walters, has seen the same thing, and for sometime we have been attempting to obtain it," says Joseph. (Walters and several others were still treasure hunting with Smith as late as the summer of 1827.)

"Joseph, what I am going to share with you must be kept in very strict confidence. I have in my possession a writing claimed to have been found in a certain mound on the frontier. I believe it could be of great worth, but could be of a greater value if it was discreetly brought to light through some marvelous manifestation. Then people would be more apt to believe in it," Rigdon tells Smith.

"Brother Rigdon, I would certainly like to see this writing," Joseph replies.

"Well, my sharing of this manuscript with you would depend upon our future relationship, but I also have other ideas of which could be of great interest to you," replies Rigdon. "Perhaps in the near future we can meet again and discuss this matter further. But, Joseph, any meeting that we might have must be carried out with as much privacy as possible," warns Rigdon.

"Yes, I have had some problems with some people wanting to know too much about my business. But, Brother Rigdon, as I have already said, I have seen gold treasures by my stone and I have often thought it might be a book of some sort. The spirit with which I have been communicating has insinuated to me that such was the case," declares Smith.

"I understand," says Rigdon, "but the manuscript I have in my possession is a tangible one. Things seen by spirits are not too likely to ever materialize. It is possible that we might incorporate what the spirit is telling you with what I have. I like the idea of an ancient manuscript coming forth as a revelation, perhaps upon gold plates, etc..."

The above is hypothetical but may not be too far from the actual reality of a discussion that might have occurred. Whether Rigdon was the Disciple preacher is not as important as the fact that the lives of Smith and Rigdon would cross, and when they did, a conversation much like the above probably took place. There were reports of Sidney Rigdon in the Palmyra vicinity in early 1827, and afterwards before the Book of Mormon was published.

Lorenzo Saunders, a resident and neighbor of the Smiths, stated:

I saw Rigdon in the spring of 1827, about the middle of

March. I went to the Smiths to eat maple sugar, and I
saw five or six men standing in a group and there was
among them better dressed than the rest and I asked
Harrison Smith who he was and he said his name was
Sidney Rigdon, a friend of Joseph's from Pennsylvania.
I saw him in the fall of 1827 on the road between where
I lived and Palmyra . . . Then in the summer of 1828 I
saw him at Samuel Lawrence's [a treasure hunting associate of Smith, as well as a possible relative] just before
the harvest. I was cutting corn for Lawrence and went to
dinner and he [Rigdon] took dinner with us and when
dinner was over they went into another room and I
didn't see him again till he came to preach in Palmyra.
(Charles A. Snook, *The True Origin of the Book of Mormon*,
p. 134)

A second witness that Rigdon was seen in Palmyra was
Abel D. Chase, a brother to the one from whom Smith
obtained his Urim and Thummin (Seer Stone). This witness
states, "I was well acquainted with the Smith family, frequently visiting the Smith boys and they me. During some of
my visits at the Smiths, I saw a stranger there who they said
was Mr. Rigdon. He was at Smiths' several times, and it was
in the year of 1827 when I first saw him there . . . Some time
after that tales were circulated that young Joe had dug or
found from the earth a book of plates . . ." (Snook, p. 131).

The third witness of seeing Rigdon was a neighbor to the
Smiths, as well as one of the proof-readers of the Book of
Mormon. His name was Pomeroy Tucker and he testifies of
the stranger appearing in Palmyra, shortly after Harris lost
the first 116 pages of the Book of Mormon. That would be
in the summer or fall of 1828. Joseph would have been in
great need to visit with Rigdon after the devastating loss of
these pages.

Back in Rigdon's home town of Mentor, Ohio, we hear
from Zebulan Rudolph, one of Rigdon's church members
and father-in-law to James A. Garfield (twentieth president
of the Unites States).

During the winter previous to the appearance of the
Book of Mormon, Rigdon was in the habit of spending
weeks away from home, going no one knew whether. He

often appeared preoccupied and he would indulge in dreamy, visionary talks, which puzzled those who listened. When the Book of Mormon appeared and Rigdon joined in the advocacy of the new religion the suspicion was at once around that he was one of the framers of the new doctrine, and probably he was not ignorant of the authorship of the Book of Mormon. (Snook, Ibid p. 151)

Recently, I visited the old Mentor congregation there in northeast Ohio, and while visiting with the present pastor, he shared with me how they still believe that when Rigdon was the Mentor pastor he was engaged in pre-Mormon activities outside of Ohio. He stated that the actions of Rigdon at that time aroused the greatest of suspicions among his (Rigdon's) members. That a secret confederacy existed between Smith and Rigdon is a conclusion unanimously agreed upon by the "Disciples."

Alexander Campbell, the Disciple Founder, wrote: "Even Sidney Rigdon told me that were Joseph to be proven a liar, or say himself that he never found the Book of Mormon as he reported, still he would believe it, and believe that all who do not believe it shall be dammed" (*Millennial Harbinger*, Vol. II, p. 332).

Oliver Cowdery, not long after severing his connection with the Mormon Church, returned to the state of Ohio, settling in Tiffin, where he practiced law and in 1840-1841 became a member of the Methodist Church. During the time that he practiced law in Tiffin, Cowdery's partner was Judge W. Lang. In the following letter addressed to Thomas Gregg of Hamilton, Illinois, author of *The Prophet of Palmyra*, this gentleman says respecting the history of Cowdery at Tiffin:

Once for all I desire to be strictly understood when I say to you that I cannot violate any confidence of a friend though he be dead [Speaking of Cowdery]. This I will say that Mr. Cowdery never spoke of his connection with the Mormons to anybody except to me. We were intimate friends. The plates were never translated and could not be, were never intended to be. What is claimed to be a translation is the *Manuscript Found* worked over by C [Cowdery]. He was the best scholar amongst them. Rigdon got the original at the job printing office in Pittsburgh as I have stated. I often expressed my objection to the frequent repetition of "and it came to pass"* to Mr. Cowdery and said that a true scholar ought to have avoided that, which only provoked a gentle smile from C [Cowdery]. Without going into detail or disclosing a confided word, I say to you that I do know, as well as can now be known, that C [Cowdery] revised the Manuscript and Smith and Rigdon approved of it before it became the Book of Mormon.

The testimonies of Lorenzo Sanders, Abel Chase, Pomeroy Tucker, and Judge Lang, as well as members of Rigdon's own congregation have provided strong evidence that Rigdon indeed was responsible for placing into Smith's hands the writing of Solomon Spaulding. This great cloud of witnesses leaves little room to doubt that the Unity Preacher of whom Lucy Smith wrote of in her memoirs was none other than Sidney Rigdon, the co-conspirator with her son, Joseph.

---

*The friends and neighbors of Solomon Spaulding in northeast Ohio gave him a nickname of "Ole Come to Pass" because the phrase appeared so often in his manuscript. In the Book of Mormon this same expression appears hundreds of times. It appears so often that the reader cannot help but notice this "strange" style of writing.

CHAPTER SIX

The Stealing
of a Manuscript

❖

The Book of Mormon had barely left the printer before a cry went up in northeast Ohio that the Mormons had plagiarized a manuscript of one Solomon Spaulding. These voices were loudly proclaiming that the Book of Mormon had not descended from the hand of an angel, but rather from the hand of one of their local residents. These voices came from Solomon Spaulding's immediate family and his close friends. They came from those who were the closest to him. There were thirteen witnesses in all which would agree that the contents of the Book of Mormon were strangely similar to what they had often heard fall from the lips of Solomon Spaulding as he had shared his writing with them, on many occasions.

Their affidavits remain to this day crying for justice against the offenders. The Mormons have debated that the manuscript Spaulding wrote carried no likeness whatsoever to the Book of Mormon, and they have strongly advocated that the controversy was without reliable base. Yet, today, there are many historians and churchmen throughout western New York, northeast Ohio, and western Pennsylvania who remain convinced that there existed a second manuscript of Solomon Spaulding altogether different, which he had titled *Manuscript Found.*

The Spaulding writing which the Mormons used to try and prove their case was called *Manuscript Story*, a manuscript which Spaulding never finished. The original of this manuscript is in the possession of Oberlin College in Oberlin, Ohio.

Solomon Spaulding left Conneaut, Ohio, in 1812 and moved to Pittsburgh, Pennsylvania. Shortly thereafter, he would place the writing of his *Manuscript Found* into the hands of the Patterson Printing Office in hopes of them publishing it. Some months later the manuscript disappeared from the printing office.

There is substantial testimony which agrees that the *Manuscript Found* of Solomon Spaulding was taken from the Patterson Printing Office in Pittsburgh, Pennsylvania. It is believed by many that the person who removed the manuscript from the print shop was Sidney Rigdon, who would later join the Disciples of Christ, and then Mormonism. He was in Pittsburgh, Pennsylvania, at the time the Spaulding manuscript came up missing. According to the witnesses, even Solomon Spaulding himself believed that Rigdon stole his manuscript.

Mrs. Eichbaum, a Pittsburgh resident, gives an eye witness testimony of Rigdon's Pittsburgh days:

> My father, John Johnson, was postmaster at Pittsburgh for about eighteen years, from 1804 to 1822. My husband, William Eichbaum, succeeded him, and was postmaster for about eleven years, from 1822 to 1833. I was born August 25, 1792, and when I became old enough, I assisted my father in attending to the post office, and became familiar with his duties. From 1811 to 1816, I was the regular clerk in the office; assorting, making up, dispatching, opening, and distributing the mails.

> Pittsburgh was then a small town, and I was well acquainted with all the stated visitors at the office who called regularly for their mails. So meager at that time were the mails that I could generally tell without looking whether or not there was anything for such persons, though I would usually look in order to satisfy them. I was married in 1815, and the next year my connection with the office ceased, except during the absences of my

husband. I knew and distinctly remember Robert and
Joseph Patterson, J. Harrison Lambdin [printer in
Patterson's shop)] Silas Engles, and Sidney Rigdon. I
remember Rev. Mr. Spaulding, but simply as one who
occasionally called to inquire for letters.

I remember there was an evident intimacy between
Lambdin and Rigdon. They very often came to the office
together. I particularly remember that they would thus
come during the hour on Sabbath afternoon when the
office was required to be open, and I remember feeling
sure that Rev. Mr. Patterson knew nothing of this, or he
would have put a stop to it. I do not know what position,
if any, Rigdon filled in Patterson's store or printing
office, but am well assured he was frequently, if not
constantly, there for a large part of the time when I was
clerk in the post office. I recall Mr. Engles saying that
"Rigdon was always hanging around the printing office."
He was connected with the tannery before he became a
preacher, though he may have continued the business
whilst preaching. (Charles A. Shook, *The True Origin of
the Book of Mormon*, p. 117-118)

Pittsburgh during the early 1800s was a small town and
had a small post office. This postal clerk would have known
everyone for miles around. It wasn't too many years ago
when it was considered a professional responsibility for the
postal clerks to personally know those whom they serviced.

It is believed that the Spaulding manuscript came up
missing sometime after the year 1815. Mrs. Eichbaum stated
that when she was old enough that she helped her father
operate the post office in Pittsburgh. She was sixteen-years-
old in the year 1808, and by 1811 she became a regular
postal clerk. Spaulding did not arrive until the year 1812,
and his manuscript was not taken until approximately three
years later. By the year 1814 Mrs. Eichbaum was twenty-two
years of age and certainly old enough to have obtained a
very good knowledge of the inhabitants of a small town. For
her to have had a distinct knowledge of Solomon Spaulding
and Sidney Rigdon would have been only normal. But we
also read of her cognizance of Rigdon spending considerable time in the very printing office where Solomon

Spaulding's *Manuscript Found* was awaiting to be published. She further implied that Rigdon's presence around the premise was suspicious, to say the least.

Two people in later years would testify that Sidney Rigdon had at one time a manuscript in his possession, long before the Book of Mormon was published. To one of these witnesses Rigdon stated that Spaulding had written it. The Mormons have gone to great lengths to try and merge the thinking concerning the *Manuscript Found* to another work of Spaulding called *Manuscript Story*. This work of sabotage was done in hopes that it would be believed by the masses that the *Manuscript Story* was in essence the stolen *Manuscript Found*. The Mormons desired for the public to believe that there was only one manuscript and that it had been given two separate titles. Today, the original *Manuscript Story* is in the archives of Oberlin College in Oberlin, Ohio.

When the Mormons reprinted *Manuscript Story* several years ago, they added to the title page in smaller print the words *Manuscript Found*, and also added the same words at the top of each succeeding page of the manuscript. But Mr. Baumann, archivist at Oberlin College, stated that the words *Manuscript Found* do not appear on the original *Manuscript Story* in his possession.

I sent Mr. Baumann a copy of the title page of *Manuscript Story* which contained the added words of *Manuscript Found* and his reply is as follows:

> Oberlin College Archives
> 420 Mudd Center
> Oberlin College
> Oberlin, Ohio 44074-1532
>
> October 14, 1992

Dear Mr. Fuller:

Thank you for the fax of the Solomon Spaulding item.

My response is as follows. The text may have been printed verbatim; yet it is likely that the publishers created a fresh and interesting title for the manuscript in order to foster sales. This is often done, especially in those cases where a title to a manuscript did not exist. Please note that "Manuscript Found" is in quotes, which often means that words were supplied.

I do not think the title page is missing. This statement is made without a check of the secondary literature bearing on the subject.

Enclosed for your use is a statement on the Spaulding Manuscript prepared by the College.

Sincerely,
Roland M. Baumann, Archivist

College Statement

This library possesses a manuscript which apparently is in the handwriting of Solomon Spaulding, since it seems to agree with fragments of account books which I have seen, and its genuineness is certified by a number of people who apparently examined it about the year 1839. It is not, however, the manuscript that was said by witnesses to resemble the Book of Mormon, since that manuscript was always spoken of as having been written in the style of the sacred scriptures, whereas this is a plain narrative containing accounts of the wars between the Kentucks and the Sciotos-Indian tribes ascribed to this country.

The manuscript which we have was apparently obtained from Spaulding's effects at West Amity, Pennsylvania, at some time after the publication of the Book of Mormon, and seems to have been found as a result of a search to find whatever remained of Spaulding's writings in order to throw light on the question of whether he was the author of the Book of Mormon, or not. The manuscript which we have was copied under our supervision and a typewritten copy furnished to the Shepherd Book Company of Salt Lake City, Utah and also to the Reorganized Church of Jesus Christ of Latter Day Saints, then located at Lamoni, Iowa. It was printed and sold by both branches of the Mormon Church, who gave it the title "Manuscript Found"—a title which does not appear in any way on the manuscript, which simply has pencilled upon the paper in which it was wrapped, "Manuscript Story, Conneaut Creek."

From the above statement from Oberlin College the reader can observe first hand how the Mormons altered the works of Solomon Spaulding so as to deceive the masses. This is evidence that the plagiarizing of the works of Spaulding by the Mormons did not stop with Smith and Rigdon.

There were several witnesses who gave convicting evidence that Rigdon and Smith made extensive use of Spaulding's work in the creation of the Book of Mormon.

1. Alexander Campbell, founder of the Disciples for Christ, said that Rigdon told him in 1827 "that the plates dug up in New York was an account, not only of the aborigines of this country, but also it was stated that the Christian religion had been preached in this country during the First Century, just as we were preaching it on the Western Reserve" (*Millennial Harbinger*, 1844). How would Rigdon have known what the plates contained; for the *Mormon History* declares that he didn't know Mormonism existed until November 1830. Who was providing Rigdon with such information, two years before the Book of Mormon was published?

2. A second witness to that same information was Rev. Adamson Bentley, Rigdon's wife's brother-in-law, who stated, "I know that Sidney Rigdon told me there was a book coming out [the manuscript which had been found on gold plates] as much as two years before the Mormon book made its appearance in this country or had been heard of by me."

These two extremely close associates of Sidney Rigdon go on record that Rigdon knew of the "plates" and of a special book to be published from them. How did Rigdon obtain such information to pass on to Bentley and Campbell? Campbell, Rigdon, and Bentley were the main leaders of the "Disciples of Christ Church" at that time in the Ohio and Pennsylvania region. There can be no other conclusion, except that Rigdon knew the source from which the Book of Mormon would spring, and would very soon be placing Spaulding's manuscript into Smith's hands.

3. Rev. John Winter, M.D., a member of Rigdon's own church and a school teacher states: "In 1822 or 1823 Rigdon took out of his desk in his study a large manuscript stating

that it was a Bible romance purporting to be a history of the American Indians. That it was written by one Spaulding, a Presbyterian preacher, whose health had failed, and who had taken it to the printers to see if it would pay to publish it, and he [Rigdon] had borrowed it from the printer as a curiosity" (*Braden & Kelley Debate*, p. 42).

4. Rigdon's wife's own niece spoke of a manuscript that Rigdon had in his possession.

> When I was quite a child I visited Mr. Rigdon's family (1826-1827). He married my aunt. They at the time lived in Bainbridge, Ohio. During my visit Mr. Rigdon went to his bedroom and took from a trunk which he kept locked a certain manuscript. He came out into the other room and seated himself by the fireplace and commenced reading it. His wife at that moment came into the room and exclaimed, "What! you're studying that thing again?" Or something to that effect. She then added, "I mean to burn that paper." He said, "No, indeed, you will not. This will be a great thing some day." Whenever he was reading this he was so completely occupied that he seemed entirely unconscious of anything passing around him." (Patterson, Jr., Solomon, *Spaulding and the Book of Mormon, History of Washington County, PA.*, p. 434)

5. Also, Spaulding's physician, Dr. Cephas Dodd, gave an amazing testimony of the manuscript saga. This doctor wrote the following on 5 June 1831 on the fly-leaf of his Book of Mormon:

> This work I am convinced by facts related to me by my deceased patient, Solomon Spaulding, has been made from writings of Spaulding, probably by Sidney Rigdon, who was suspicioned by Spaulding with purloining his manuscript from the publishing house to which he had taken it; and I am prepared to testify that Spaulding told me that his work was entitled, *The Manuscript Found in the Wilds of Mormon: or Unearthed Records of the Nephites*. From his description of its contents, I fully believe that this Book of Mormon is mainly and wickedly copied from it. (Cowdrey, Davis, Scales, *Who Really Wrote the Book of Mormon*, p. 100)

6. Dr. J. C. Bennett, the mayor of Nauvoo, who was expelled from the Mormon Church by Smith, states in 1842,

> I will remark here . . . that the Book of Mormon was originally written by the Rev. Solomon Spaulding, A.M., as a romance, and entitled the *Manuscript Found*, and placed by him in the printing-office of Patterson and Lambdin, in the city of Pittsburgh, from whence it was taken by a conspicuous Mormon divine [Rigdon], and re-modeled, by adding the religious portion, placed by him in Smith's possession, and then published to the world as the testimony exemplifies. This I have from the Confederation [Joseph, Hyrum, and Sidney], and of its perfect correctness there is not a shadow of a doubt. There never were any plates of the Book of Mormon, excepting what were seen by the spiritual, and not the natural eyes of the witnesses. The story of the plates is all chimerical. . . .

7. (Sarah) Pratt, the wife of an early Mormon leader, testified to the veracity of Bennett's statements: Salt Lake City, March 31, 1886: "This certifies that I was well acquainted with the Mormon Leaders and church in general, and know that the principal statements in John C. Bennett's book on Mormonism are true." (Ibid, pp. 102-103)

The above testimonies were from a very diverse group of people, some of whom were very reputable, and others were at one time personal friends of either Smith or Spaulding. In the collection above are two ministers, one mayor, two doctors, and Rigdon's wife's own niece. Together their testimonies produce irrefutable evidence of Rigdon as being the prime suspect of having taken the Spaulding manuscript.

Not only did the Spauldings touch early Mormonism through deeds of Rigdon, but years before this, their lives were touching the Smiths in ways and places the Mormons have never told.

CHAPTER SEVEN

What Vermont's Green Mountains Can't Tell

❖

Solomon Spaulding's good friend, Ethan Smith, published a book in 1823 called *View of the Hebrews*. This book attempted to show that the American Indian was a descendant of the lost tribes of the House of Israel. A substantial part of this book appears in varying ways in the Book of Mormon. We show some of these likenesses in a later chapter. But in the following chapters, information will be presented that will throw light upon the relationships of Ethan and Solomon, as well as upon the Spauldings and the First Mormon founders. The Mormons have been absolutely silent on these old acquaintances between the Solomon Spaulding, the Joseph Smith, and the Oliver Cowdery families.

Solomon Spaulding, author of *Manuscript Found*, was born in Ashford, Connecticut, in 1761 and graduated from Dartmouth College in 1785, but remained in the area and received his license of ordination in 1787 as a Congregational Minister (Rev. George T. Chapman, *Sketches Of The Alumni of Dartmouth College*). Solomon continued his studies after graduation, and it was during this time, according to Ethan's grandson, that he and Ethan Smith became close friends. They could have shared some courses together there at Dartmouth. Solomon would remain in the northeast preaching, etc., until some time after 1894 according to Dartmouth records. This was four years after Ethan Smith's graduation from Dartmouth.

Since both were Congregational ministers and shared the same professors, it is very certain that Ethan Smith and Solomon Spaulding knew each other very well. One of the grandsons of Ethan Smith wrote that Solomon Spaulding and Ethan were very close friends and continued to be over the years, and that there was a definite perusing of Ethan's works by Spaulding (*Cleveland Plain Dealer*, 24 April 1887). This would certainly have given many opportunities for Spaulding and Ethan Smith to share their theories and beliefs relative to the origin of the American Indians. Both men probably were an inspiration one to another. But their common interest in the history of the origin of the American Indians would have been a strong motivation to keep their friendship fresh for a number of years.

I would venture to say that because of sharing their views together that many similarities would have existed between the *View of the Hebrews*, written by Ethan Smith, and Spaulding's work, *Manuscript Found*.

During the years that Solomon's health was failing, as well as his business, his friend Ethan may have shared his thoughts and writings very extensively with Solomon, so as to help him. Solomon stated himself that he needed to get the *Manuscript Found* published for monetary reasons. Since the Book of Mormon has interwined throughout its pages ideas, concepts, and partial quotations which are indeed very harmonious to Ethan Smith's *View of the Hebrews*, it carries good reason that Spaulding did receive help with his work, *Manuscript Found*, from his dear friend.

For several years in and around Poultney, Vermont, the home of Ethan Smith, there lived many relatives of Solomon Spaulding. Orrin Spaulding, son of Nathaniel, moved into Danby in 1794 and then into the Poultney-Middletown, Vermont, area. He apparently was in the group with Joseph, Asahel, Julius, George, and Reuben, whom previously had lived in Plainfield, Connecticut, the original home of Solomon's father. Reuben Spaulding, Jr., was most likely the son of Reuben Spaulding, Solomon Spaulding's uncle.

Solomon had an older brother named Reuben, who was no doubt named after his uncle. This brother was born in Plainfield, Connecticut, along with his sister Priscilla. Solomon and the rest of his brothers and sisters were born in Ashford, Connecticut, where his father, Josiah, moved the family in 1760.

Joseph Spaulding helped start the Congregational Church of Middletown, Vermont. This was just a few miles from Poultney where Ethan Smith would later pastor the Congregational Church. Azel Spaulding, Solomon's first cousin, was probably the Asahel Spaulding mentioned in the *History of Middletown, Vermont*.

There are some very interesting marriage connections which were created in Vermont, which could provide information that could easily travel from the doorstep of Solomon Spaulding to the doorstep of Joseph and Lucy Smith.

One example is Reuben Spaulding, Solomon Spaulding's uncle, who married Mary Pierce in 1747. She died in Sharon, Vermont (Joseph Smith's hometown), in 1826, having lived there for many years. Her daughter Mary married Ebenezer Parkhurst, resident of Sharon, Vermont. They had nine children and were neighbors of the Joseph Smith family. Here we have the Smiths living for several years alongside Solomon's first cousin, Mary Parkhurst. Back in the days when families took pride in family members being educated, Solomon would certainly have been a subject of pride to Mary. Also, the Smiths came from a "congregational" background, of which Spaulding was an ordained minister.

The Smiths once lived in Tunbridge, Vermont (near Sharon), a little town about ten miles south of Chelsea. In the year 1787 Solomon Spaulding's brother, Elisha Spaulding, settled in Chelsea. All eight of his children were born there. He named one of his sons Solomon, in honor of his brother. These Spauldings continued to reside in Chelsea until 1823 when they moved to Ohio. The possibility of Spaulding's brother, Elisha, meeting the Smiths is great indeed, considering he also had a first cousin, Reuben, living in the town of Sharon, Vermont.

This Reuben Spaulding was also Solomon Spaulding's first cousin. He raised his entire family in Sharon, Vermont.

They moved into Sharon ten to twelve years before Joseph,
Sr., and Lucy Mack Smith. Jerusha Spaulding (Reuben's wife)
raised twelve children and had several children equal in ages
to the Smith children. Their son Levi was born in September
1805, approximately three-and-a-half months before Joseph
Smith, Jr., was born, Lucy being approximately six months
pregnant with Joseph when Levi was born.

Sharon is a very tiny town; my wife and I were there
recently. In the town there were two shops, one restaurant,
one gas station, and a small post office. The Smiths and the
Spauldings spent several years together in such a small community. Back in those days people would want to know
where you came from, and all about you. Lucy Smith and
Jerusha Spaulding had plenty to talk about of such things,
since both of their families were from Connecticut, and both
were expecting an 1805 child.

I would suspect that before Solomon made his way west
that he probably paid his relatives a visit there in Sharon and
Chelsea. The Smiths may have even had the privilege of
meeting Solomon Spaulding. But if they did not, it would be
a definite forgone assumption that the name of Solomon
was brought up in conversation on many occasions over the
years. The Solomon name would have attracted Lucy Smith's
attention since that was the name of her father.

Solomon would have been living in Conneaut, Ohio, in
the year 1805, the year of Joseph and Levi's birth, and
probably would have been working on his manuscript at that
time. Perhaps Solomon was motivated to name the first
leading character of his manuscript Levi in thought of his
nephew Levi. One relative wrote in her book that Solomon
had used the name Levi in his manuscript, instead of Lehi.

Since the Smiths did not leave the Sharon area until the
year of Solomon's death in 1816, they could have easily
learned of Solomon's movements to Pittsburgh and his intent to publish his "works", *Manuscript Found*. They also
could have learned that it had been stolen and that one
Sidney Rigdon was suspect in the loss.

Joseph would have been only an interested ten–year–old
at this time, but his parents certainly could have taken notice
to these things. Levi and his brothers would have been friends

and schoolmates of Joseph and could have spent many afternoons in play together. The name Spaulding would have certainly stuck in Joseph's memory forever. Yet, neither Joseph, Jr., or Lucy Mack Smith, his mother, in writing of his childhood ever mention the name Spaulding. But no doubt that day when Rigdon told him that he had the manuscript written by Spaulding, memories of those years began to flood his mind. Particularly that day in 1816 when they departed the Sharon-Norwich area, and Joseph was bidding his friends good-bye, little Levi Spaulding would probably be the one whom he would miss the most. I wonder what went through Joseph's mind a few years later as he was plagiarizing the manuscript of one of the relatives of his little friend Levi.

There was also a Jacob Smith, who was in Ethan Smith's graduating class of 1790 from Dartmouth, having a law practice in Royalton, Vermont, from 1800 to 1812. The Smiths actually lived closer to Royalton than they did Sharon, and at one time lived in Royalton during the years that Jacob Smith had his practice there.

In the town of Poultney, Vermont, some of the Spauldings were members of the Congregational Church and were probably good friends with the Congregational pastor, Ethan Smith, author of *The View of the Hebrews*. The relatives of Solomon could offer Ethan many opportunities to have discussed the life and the problems of Solomon. Being a nephew to Solomon could have caused Reuben Spaulding, Jr., to take considerable interest in Ethan Smith. He could have been one close means of conveying the work of Solomon to both Ethan and the Cowderys.

During those times there lived in Wells and Poultney, Vermont, the Spauldings, Pratts, Cowderys, Fullers, Spragues, Lewises, Hales, with the Brigham Young family not far away. This same list can be repeated for the Sharon, Royalton, and Tunbridge, Vermont areas. What one might conclude is that what happened in Wells, Middletown, or Poultney was known in Sharon and Royalton; and then what was occurring in Royalton and Sharon would soon be known in Poultney, Wells, and Middletown. We might as well add Hartford, New York, the home of the Pratts (Parley and Orson), which was just ten miles from Wells, Vermont. John Pratt (Parley's relative) was living in Wells, having moved over from Hartford, New York. Also the news went on to Jeremiah Pratt who at that time lived near the Smith family at Sharon, Vermont.

This John Pratt was probably the Pratt listed in the *History of Wells* who was involved in the "Woods' Religious Movement," which William Cowdery, Jr., and Joseph Smith, Sr., were very prominent in.

What is truly interesting is that both Joseph Smith, Jr., and Oliver Cowdery, as well as Parley Pratt, were raised with close relatives of Solomon Spaulding, and probably were classmates with many of them.

What we do know for certain is that both Ethan Smith and Solomon Spaulding graduated from Dartmouth College. Both were Congregational ministers. Both had great interest in the origin of the American Indians. Both were good friends, according to Ethan Smith's grandson. Both are considered as having contributed substantively to the Book of Mormon.

Perhaps, Ethan Smith was aware that his good friend Solomon Spaulding had died in 1816 failing to have published his works. He probably felt that the work they had done need not go unpublished. Therefore, in 1823 in Poultney, Vermont, Ethan Smith published his first edition of the *View of the Hebrews*. In 1825 he published his second edition.

Oliver Cowdery was living in Poultney, Vermont, at this time and some of his sisters had previously been baptized into the Congregational Church. This was also the church of his step-mother. This may be enough to assume that Oliver gave attendance to the church from time to time. Ethan Smith was pastor of the Congregational Church in Poultney from 21 November 1821 to December 1826 (Alumni Records, Dartmouth College, 1790).

It is very possible that Oliver knew Reverend Smith personally, and when he left Poultney for Palmyra in 1825 he had a copy of the *View of the Hebrews* in his possession. It is very possible that Ethan shared with Oliver concerning his friend, Solomon Spaulding, or Cowdery may have learned about them from the Spaulding's relatives that he had grown up with.

It is not beyond possibility that before Ethan died that he had heard of Sidney Rigdon and the vanishing of Solomon's *Manuscript Found.* He could have learned of Rigdon's theft by Solomon himself, or by one of Spaulding's close relatives. Before Cowdery left Poultney in 1825 Ethan could have mentioned Rigdon's name to him. Oliver Cowdery, having lived so long among the Spauldings, could have easily passed on some interesting information to his cousin, Joseph Smith, upon his relocation to New York in 1825. During his trip to Kirtland in 1826, Oliver, upon hearing that Sidney Rigdon was nearby, could with great intrigue desired to meet such an infamous character.

Although Oliver Cowdery was to play a prominent part in the Book of Mormon conspiracy, of which later he lived to regret, it becomes obvious that his dreams of a special place in the Mormon Kingdom, for which he diligently labored, would come to a frustrating end, only ten years after it all began. Among the Mormons of his day he would always be remembered as the "sheep who went astray."

CHAPTER EIGHT

The Mormon Sheep That Went Astray

❖

Oliver Cowdery was one of the early Mormons' most renowned leaders. He was surpassed in popularity only by Brigham Young and Joseph Smith. This man would stay at the side of Smith for seven years. He was one man who on several occasions would openly disagree with the Mormon prophet. But the Mormons have never revealed much about this man's background, except that when he met Smith in 1829 they were both strangers.

When the winds of polygamy, along with the fanning of the wings of Smith's avenging angels, began to stir, it was more than Cowdery could take. His conscience allowed him to go no further. When Cowdery challenged Smith's unscriptural practices, he was cut off from the Church and later would have to flee for his life.

Oliver Cowdery became a famous Mormon for two reasons. The first being he was the most noted scribe for Smith in the writing of the Book of Mormon. Secondly, he would become one of the Book of Mormon's famous witnesses. Although he figured very prominently in the rise of Mormonism, their later history books are suspiciously silent concerning him. They all but ignore the life of Cowdery in the five years preceding the publishing of the Book of Mormon.

Suddenly, in Mormon history, Cowdery appears in Palmyra in the year 1829 where he takes a job as a school teacher for one week. Whereupon, he resigns and immediately heads for Harmony, Pennsylvania (near Binghamton, New York), to become Smith's scribe. According to one Mormon source Cowdery arrived in Harmony in early April, and they began work on the Book of Mormon 17 April 1829. This date is probably the more accurate one, since Lucy Smith states that it was in April when Cowdery departed Palmyra, and he would stop for a visit with the Whitmers on his way down to Pennsylvania.

On page 145 of volume one of the *RLDS Mormon History* it states that the Book of Mormon was completed in fifty days, before 11 June 1829, save a few pages.

One year earlier when Emma Smith and Martin Harris were scribing the first 116 pages for Smith, they could only scribe one page per day. But Cowdery comes on the scene, and he and Smith are able to scribe *fifteen pages* per day. The whole process speeds up fifteen times. If a typist could type 150-words-a-minute and was to suddenly increase to 2,250-words-a-minute, somebody would be asking for an explanation. What could have created such phenomenal increase in the volume of pages scribed?

Since Cowdery was so eager to rush down to see Smith, it leads one to the conclusion that he had in his possession something that Smith was anxiously awaiting. Cowdery's sudden resignation after only one week of teaching increases the suspicion that he had in hand the final reworked version of Spaulding's manuscript. To accelerate the translation by fifteen times, is sufficient evidence in itself that the homework had been done.

It had been almost one year since losing the first 116 pages of the original work, the loss of which had put Smith in great straits. For upon learning of it Joseph exclaimed, "Oh, my God, all is lost! What shall I do?" (Fawn Brodie, *No Man Knows My History*, p. 54).

Fear had set in on Joseph. The possibility of the truth of his conjured-up deception would create the worst possible embarrassment. He was afraid to re-duplicate the 116 pages as it might expose him, so he designs a revelation that there exists in his collection another "set of plates." He and God's argument were that if he retranslated the plates from which the "lost" 116 pages were produced, his enemies (Martin Harris' wife and etc.) would alter his words and publish them. This was ridiculous since a reproduction would prove to validate, not incriminate Joseph. The truth was he knew he could not recreate the same identical information. Smith knew he had injected too much of his own imagination into it. It seems very probable that Smith did not have a fully written manuscript in front of him for the first 116 pages. Plus he apparently had included a great deal of anti-Masonic material in the "lost" 116 pages.

Joseph's excuse for not commencing on with the translation was that he had to go to work, as well as, claiming the Lord had taken the Urim and Thummin away from him. Yet he still had the "seer stone" in his pocket which Emma said he used to translate the book (*RLDS Church History*, Vol. III). All the early Mormons, along with the three witnesses Cowdery, Whitmer, and Harris, agreed with Emma on this method of translation. Since Smith was able to translate with the plates hid off in the woods by using his "seer stone," then it becomes obvious that the "Nephite instruments" were just another diversionary ingredient in his fairy tale. Joseph probably figured that such an excuse would fair quite well. To the "sheep" which followed him, anything Smith said, and that God said, was surely heaven's most holy light.

Joseph and company had several months to ponder over losing the 116 pages of the manuscript and try to come up with a solution to his embarrassing dilemma. Of course, according to Smith, there was God's power to strike you dead if you looked at the plates, but not enough of God's power to prevent the loss of 116 pages nor to quickly remedy Smith's grave situation. One would think God certainly had some responsibility in the matter since He was the one who, according to Smith, had called him to this job. God had slipped up it seems!

Oliver Cowdery may have just been the "man on the spot." The word "Oliver" means a trip hammer—operated by

the foot. Oliver becomes Joseph's "trip hammer" and starts
the action rolling again. He strangely arrives in Palmyra, as
it first appears, to accept a respectable job of school teaching. But this was obviously a diversionary scheme all along,
since Hyrum Smith (Joseph's brother) was one of the trust-
ees of the school. Cowdery's pretensions of teaching school
very quickly dissipated, as he now learns what everyone else
knew, which was that Smith was down in Pennsylvania several miles to the south, engaged in a secretive work for God.

According to Lucy Smith, Oliver's "curiosity" became so
strong that he asked Hyrum Smith to be relieved of his
duties after one week as school master, and with no resistance from Hyrum he sets out for Harmony, Pennsylvania,
on a cold wet snowy day in April (Lucy Mack Smith, *Joseph
Smith the Prophet And His Progenitors*, p. 130). Joseph, at the
same moment over one hundred miles away, just happened
to look into his "crystal ball" (seer stone), and saw Oliver on
his way and knew immediately that his answer for a scribe
had come. Smith and all the Mormons claim that this was
the first time he and Cowdery had met.

Perhaps some of the mystery surrounding Oliver Cowdery
can be removed. The problem one encounters when you
study Mormon history is that you will find at your disposal
volumes of material about things they wish you to know, and
only scant materials of those things they desire not to have
known. This is true of Oliver Cowdery's few years from 1822
to 1829. Their account of Oliver is that he suddenly appears
in 1829. Little or nothing is printed of those years between
1822-29; although Inez Davis, one Mormon author, does
mention that Oliver was in Palmyra in 1828.

David Whitmer, one of the three witnesses to the Book
of Mormon, said that he met Oliver in Palmyra several months
before Oliver goes to scribe for Smith, and he also said that
Oliver stopped by to see him before going on down to the
Smiths at Harmony, Pennsylvania. His stopping could have
been to call on David Whitmer's young sister, who would
later become Cowdery's wife.

There is one "gentile" source which was aware of Oliver's
coming to Palymra in 1826 to teach school, and then leaving

for the summer and returning the following year a short
while before joining with Joseph Smith. He states,

> As respecting Oliver Cowdery, he came from Kirtland in
> the summer of 1826, and was there until fall and took a
> school in the district where the Smiths lived. And the
> next summer he was missing and I didn't see him until
> fall and he came back and took our school in the district
> where we lived and taught about a week and went to the
> schoolboard and wanted the board to let him off—and
> they did—he went to Smith and went to writing the Book
> of Mormon, Lorenzo Saunders. (Charles A. Shook, *The
> True Origin of the Book of Mormon*, p. 135)

Mr. Saunders could have been one year off concerning
Cowdery's coming from Kirtland and beginning his teaching
in Palmyra. Cowdery could have gone to Kirtland in the fall
of 1826 and returned sometime in the spring of 1827.

The Mormons tell the story that Oliver was teaching in
the spring of 1829 before going to join Smith. Lorenzo
Saunders, a local resident of the Palmyra area, stated that
Cowdery began his teaching in the fall of 1827 (probably
1828) for one week before joining Smith. The date of 1828
would leave a discrepancy of some six months between what
the Mormons tell and what a local residence witnessed. It
appears more to reason that Cowdery would have begun his
teaching in the fall rather than the spring. What Lorenzo
Saunders stated about Oliver is verified in Mormon history
except the portion about Oliver being in Kirtland in 1826.
If Oliver was in Kirtland in 1826, this could have been the
time that Cowdery would have made his acquaintance with
Sidney Rigdon. The Mormons, if they knew this information
regarding Cowdery, would not want it divulged.

Rigdon had moved to Geauga County, Ohio, in the spring
of 1826 as reported on page 191 in the *History of Disciples*.
Rigdon soon began pastoring a Campbellite Church only
four miles from Kirtland, Ohio, and gave ministry in Kirtland
itself. If what Mr. Saunders says of Oliver is true, which
cannot be disputed, then Oliver's presence in Kirtland could
have resulted in his going with his friend Parley Pratt to help
Parley build his log cabin.

A Closer Look at This Man Cowdery

Approximately two years after Oliver left Vermont in 1825, we learn that he is teaching school in the Palmyra area and is living with Lucy and Joseph Smith, Sr., (keeping in mind that Oliver had been living in the adjoining township which could have put the Smiths and Cowderys only three or four miles from each other). Oliver Cowdery is spoken of in all of the Mormon writings as a "stranger" who came upon the scene just in the nick of time to help Joseph write the Book of Mormon. But the facts regarding Oliver Cowdery will bring a great deal of understanding as to why the Mormons have written so little about this man.

Shortly before joining Smith in Pennsylvania, Oliver was teaching school and living with the Joseph Smith, Sr., family in the Palmyra area. Lucy Mack Smith (Joseph's mother) at this time writes in her book of a statement Cowdery made to her when he was told that he would have to find a residence elsewhere, as the Smiths were being forced to move. Oliver's reply to Mrs. Smith was, "'Mother', exclaimed the young man, 'let me stay with you, for I can live in any log hut where you and father live, but I cannot leave you, so do not mention it'" (Lucy Mack Smith, *Joseph Smith: The Prophet and His Progenitors*, p. 130). This is a very interesting comment for a stranger to make!

Why would Oliver have called Lucy "mother" and Joseph, Sr., "father"? The answer is simple; the family of Lucy (Gates) Mack Smith had known the Cowderys before the Vermont days, for some three or four generations previous. The Gates, Cowderys, and Fullers were all neighbors down in East Haddam, Connecticut. Oliver Cowdery's great-grandfather, John Fuller, and Lucy (Gates) Mack Smith's great-grandfather, Shubael Fuller, were brothers. It follows:

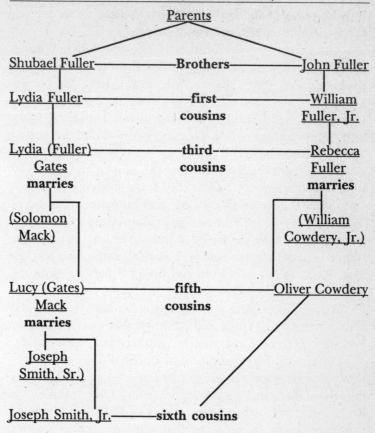

Parents

Shubael Fuller————————Brothers————————John Fuller

Lydia Fuller————————first————————William
cousins Fuller, Jr.

Lydia (Fuller)————————third————————Rebecca
Gates cousins Fuller
marries marries

(Solomon (William
Mack) Cowdery, Jr.)

Lucy (Gates)————————fifth————————Oliver Cowdery
Mack cousins
marries

Joseph
Smith, Sr.)

Joseph Smith, Jr.————sixth cousins

In 1760 Lucy (Gates) Mack's father, Solomon Mack,
married Lydia (Fuller) Gates in East Haddam, Connecticut.
In 1787 William Cowdery, Jr., Oliver's father, married Re-
becca Fuller in East Haddam, Connecticut. Lydia Gates
(Fuller) Mack, Lucy's mother, had been living with Lucy and
Joseph Smith, Sr., up to the time they left Vermont in 1816
for New York. Lydia had been raised with the Cowderys in
Connecticut, and she would have had the Smith family well
informed of their Fuller ties. Oliver's mother, Rebecca, was
Lydia's third cousin, making their fathers first cousins. Both
Oliver and Lucy had been well informed of their family ties.

Also Nathaniel Cowdery, Jr., Oliver's great-uncle, married Lucy Mack Smith's second cousin, Mary Gates. Remem-
bering that Lucy Mack's mother was Lydia (Fuller) Gates,

thus Mary Gates and Lydia were first cousins, so we see that Lucy's second cousin marries a Cowdery.

Ansel Cowdery, the brother to Oliver's father, William, Jr., (Oliver's uncle), was living in Woodstock, Vermont, only thirteen miles from Sharon, Vermont, where Joseph was born. Also there were Cowderys living in Tunbridge, Vermont, where the Smiths had once lived. Tunbridge being only a few minutes from Sharon, Vermont, where Joseph Smith, Jr., was born.

So we learn from all this that the Smiths and Cowderys were not strangers after all, as the Mormons desire to preach. But rather they were a very close and intimate family. So on that April day in 1829 when Oliver showed up in Harmony, Pennsylvania, to be the scribe of Joseph, he was *not a stranger*, rather he was Joseph's cousin. The relationship was so close that Oliver felt at liberty to call Joseph's parents "mother" and "father."

What it all boils down to is: Joseph's maternal grandfather married a half-Fuller and Oliver's father married a Fuller, and they were both married in East Haddam, Connecticut.

Oliver was living amidst his kinfolks! This would certainly be one good reason to call Lucy "mother." I am certain that Oliver was comforted in calling Lucy "mother," as he had lost his own mother at the age of four. Upon his mother's death, he went to live with his mother's sister, Huldah Fuller Glass, only to see her pass away when he was eleven years of age. There existed without doubt an inner need within Oliver to call Lucy "mother." To call a strange person of whom you barely know "mother," as well as a strange man "father," NO! But to call a close long time family relative mother and father, YES!

As close as these ties may have been between Joseph and Oliver, they would not last. Great differences would develop between them and their friendship would fall apart.

Oliver wrote a little book in his own defense after he was chased out of Mormonism by his cousin Joseph. In 1839 Oliver says that the Lord Jesus told him that He did not give Joseph any revelations. That means, according to Oliver, that there were no authentic visions, no true angels, no sacred record given by God. Obviously this is what he meant when he renounced the Book of Mormon in Tiffin, Ohio. Keep in mind though that Oliver Cowdery's name, to this day, appears in the front of every Book of Mormon as a witness of its truthfulness.

We should remember that it was 150 years ago when he publicly renounced the Book of Mormon. That renouncement is not available in Mormon histories for the average lay person to read. Therefore, we desire that the reader should have the privilege of reading this account himself of Oliver's denial of the Book of Mormon. It reads as follows:

> . . . In a few years Mr. Cowdery opened a law office in Tiffin, and soon effected a partnership with Joel W. Wilson.

> In a few years Mr. Cowdery expressed a desire to associate himself with a Methodist Protestant church of this city. Rev. John Souder and myself were appointed a committee to wait on Mr. Cowdery and confer with him respecting his connection with Mormonism and the Book of Mormon . . .

> He replied that he had objections; that, in the first place, it could do no good; that he had known several to do so and they always regretted it. And, in the second place, it would have a tendency to draw public attention, invite criticism, and bring him into contempt.

> "But," said he, "nevertheless, if the church require it, I will submit to it, but I authorize and desire you and the church to publish and make known my recantation."

> We did not demand it, but submitted his name to the church, and he was unanimously admitted a member thereof.

> At that time he arose and addressed the audience present, admitted his error and implored forgiveness, and said he was sorry and ashamed of his connection with Mormonism.

> He continued his membership while he resided in Tiffin, and became superintendent of the Sabbath-school, and led an exemplary life while he resided with us . . . (Signed) G. J. Keen.

Sworn to before me and subscribed in my presence, this
14th day of April, A. D. 1885 Frank L. Emich, Notary
Public in Seneca, O. (Charles A. Shook, *The True Origin
of the Book of Mormon*, pp. 58-59)

Oliver was the Second Elder of the Mormon Church and
one of the three witness of the Book of Mormon; certainly
one of Mormonism's founding pillars. (He was later to be
called by Joseph Smith a liar, counterfeiter, adulterer, etc.)
After he was driven out of Mormonism he had to be careful
of what he divulged. He already was under a death threat
from Joseph Smith's Danites (Avenging Angels), but to make
public that he had been a party to the Spaulding manuscript
would have put him in serious trouble with many of the
inhabitants of Ohio and could have easily affected his law
practice there at Tiffin. But the greater danger which he may
have feared, if he allowed too much to surface, would be the
reaction from the Mormon leaders themselves, who had
already branded him as the "worst of traitors." He had a
family with young children and no doubt was wanting a
normal peaceful home for them.

Oliver, by denying the truthfulness of the Book of Mormon, opens the door wide to conclude that his shady trip to
Harmony was but for the set purpose to place within Smith's
hands the reworked manuscript of Spaulding. But what
appears to have taken place before the Harmony trip was
that for several weeks he, Smith, and Rigdon had enter-
tained meetings for the purpose of solving the dilemma
created by the "lost" 116 pages and putting the manuscript
into final scribing order.

In 1839 Oliver made a bold effort to expose the whole
sham without fully indicting himself. He wrote of the angel
meeting he and Smith had in the woods (This meeting was
in the woods of Harmony, Pennsylvania, approximately
twenty-five miles from Binghamton, New York.) to bestow
upon them the "Priesthood of Aaron." The angel said that
he was John the Baptist, but later Cowdery would write that
the angel sounded like Sidney Rigdon. This statement was
made by Cowdery after he and Smith crossed swords in

Missouri and Joseph had put the "Danites"* on Oliver's trail. The angel was beyond a shadow of a doubt Rigdon since this appearance took place 15 May 1829, approximately the time when Smith and Cowdery would have the Book of Mormon about half completed. Also this fits perfectly into one of the major gaps in Rigdon's ministerial itinerary while still a Disciple pastor.

Cowdery's participation in the Mormon scheme would cover a period of approximately ten years. He would outlive his cousin Joseph by six years. Oliver Cowdery would die of tuberculosis in Richmond, Missouri, in 1850.

---

*The "Danites" were a secret band of men organized by Smith and Rigdon for the purpose of performing acts which Smith deemed necessary against the inhabitants of Missouri, as well as dissenters among his own people. Many of the acts which were committed were not only unlawful, but represented a character which would sicken the hearts of decent Christians. The Danites later would be known as the Avenging Angels both in Missouri and Utah. The "Avenging Angels" were formed from a revelation given to Smith where it stated that God wanted them to avenge Him of His enemies. Therefore, Smith's enemies automatically became God's enemies (RLDS D&C, Sec. 98:7).

CHAPTER NINE

The Pied Piper of Mormonism

❖

In 1828 Sidney Rigdon would convert a free thinker like himself to the Unity Gospel of the Disciples of Christ. His name was Parley P. Pratt. Pratt was quickly ordained as a minister in Rigdon's organization. Somehow, in a very short period of time, as would seem, he earned himself a prestigious spot at Rigdon's side.

Parley comes from the Pratt family which had very close ties to the Cowderys and Smiths during the Vermont years. Pratt probably had the distinguished privilege of introducing Oliver Cowdery to Sidney Rigdon at some point and time. He has been suspected by many non-Mormons as the one who introduced Sidney Rigdon to Joseph Smith. Between 1829 and up until the fall of 1830 Parley would play a unique role in the developing scheme of Mormonism.

The Pratts originally migrated to New York from New Haven, Connecticut. Parley was born in Burlington, New York, in September 1807 into the family of Jared and Sarah Pratt. While Parley was still a youngster, his father Jared moved his family to Hartford in extreme eastern New York, only ten miles from Oliver Cowdery's birthplace. The movement to Hartford must have resulted from the fact that several of Jared's relatives were living there.

John Pratt, Jared's uncle, had been living in Hartford, but had moved over to Wells, Vermont, just prior to their coming. Wells is approximately eight to ten miles east of Hartford. John Pratt was living in Wells during the time of the Woods' scrape in 1800-1801 and was probably the Pratt that was named in the Woods' Movement.

History of the Town of Wells, Vermont, by Grace Pemberwood, states, "John Pratt from Hartford, New York, married Betty Scofield. They resided on 'Butts Hill'." This John Pratt had his home not more than a mile from the home of William Cowdery, Oliver's father. This gave Oliver Cowdery great opportunity to become friends with the Pratts. This closeness between the Pratts and Cowderys is reflected in the following: "In 1823 Oliver's first cousin, also named William, went to live with John Pratt, Parley P.'s great uncle, which at the time had moved to Woodstock, Vermont. William Cowdery was eight years old when the Pratts took him in" (*Genealogy of Cowdrey, William Cowdrey of Lynn, 1630 and His Descendants*). Woodstock is twelve miles from Sharon, Vermont, where Joseph Smith was born.

There is little doubt that Oliver had met Parley when they were boys between the years of 1812 and 1820 and had become good friends. They grew up only an hour from each other, and Parley's great-uncle, John Pratt, was living next door to the Cowderys in Wells. Thomas Pratt, John's son, was also living in Wells during the Cowdery sojourn. He would have been Parley's third cousin.

When the background of Oliver and Parley is brought into perspective it is not hard to understand why Parley Pratt in 1830 got off the boat at Newark, New York, just eight or nine miles from Palmyra and made his way to Hyrum Smith, Joseph's brother. Hyrum immediately took Parley to see Oliver Cowdery at Fayette, New York. The next day on 1 September 1830, Pratt was baptized by Oliver Cowdery. This episode is interesting indeed, when Pratt just the day before was holding meetings as a Unity preacher for the Disciples of Christ.

Let us go back to the year 1826. Oliver Cowdery was now living in the Newark, Palmyra-Manchester, New York, area. Parley is now a "tin peddler" passing through the area traveling the Old Indian Trail, heading west where he finds a choice spot to build a cabin near Mentor, in northeast Ohio (*The Archer of Paradise*, Reva Stanley, p. 34). I can't think of any reason why Pratt would not stop to see his old friend Oliver Cowdery, as he was passing through. Maybe this was the reason (as has been reported), that Oliver was in the Kirtland-Mentor, Ohio, area in 1826.

Oliver could easily have gone with Parley to spend some time with his old friend. Oliver could have spent several months out there making an acquaintance with Sidney Rigdon, who a few months prior had begun to minister there. This would give Rigdon, Pratt, and Cowdery time to talk over the events in Palmyra, as well as some of the rumors Cowdery may have heard about Rigdon before leaving the state of Vermont (rumors of stealing Spaulding's manuscript). Also Cowdery could have conveyed some interesting information concerning his cousin Joseph which could have caught Rigdon's ear.

The topic of Smith's seership and his recent trial would have made for very interesting conversation. Perhaps Cowdery extended an invitation to Rigdon to come to Palmyra and preach. It would give him an excellent opportunity to meet his cousin Smith. This would answer why Rigdon was in Palmyra as was earlier stated, holding meetings of which the Smiths attended. It would have been almost impossible for Cowdery to have been in the Mentor area back in those days and not to have met Sidney Rigdon.

Sidney, according to the Disciples of Christ history, had moved into that area in the spring of 1826, some six months before Pratt and Cowdery would have arrived. Dr. Horace Eaton, who lived in Palmyra at the same time the Smiths were living there, states concerning Pratt, "There was a ubiquitous tin peddler in those days by the name of Parley P. Pratt. He knew everybody in Western New York and Northern Ohio. Perhaps Pratt was the carrier-vulture who told Rigdon of the Money digger, Smith."

Rigdon was reported as being seen at the Smiths in the spring of 1827. It is highly probable that from these discussions with Pratt and Cowdery, Rigdon became convinced that Smith may well be his man! Rigdon very likely clothed

his Palmyra trip in the spring of 1827 in the guise of a
missionary one. This may give us the real clue as to why
Rigdon was to send Pratt on a mission into the same area
just three years later, and would on that same day be ordained into the new Mormon priesthood.

The Pratts were to remain near the Cowderys in eastern
New York until 1820, when they moved down to Canaan. It
was at this time that William Cowdery took most of his
family to the Palmyra, New York, area just four to six miles
from the Joseph Smith family. Oliver had gone to live with
his mother's sister, Huldah (Fuller) Glass, and did not come
to the Palmyra area until approximately 1825. This is three
to four years earlier than the Mormons like to have people
know. Although his father claimed him in the 1820 census,
Oliver did not arrive until a few years later according to
Vermont sources. From the *History of Wells, Vermont*, p. 79,
we read, "We well remember this same Oliver Cowdery
when in our boyhood, the person who was figured so largely
in giving the world the wonderful revelations that many
dupes seek to follow. He attended school in the district
where we reside in 1821 and 1822."

Oliver and Joseph were blood-kin and Joseph, Sr., and
William Cowdery were in the Woods' scrape together with
one of the Pratts; this goes to show that all three of these
families shared bonds much closer than the Mormon leaders
have been willing to confess. The Pratts without question
knew the Cowderys and the Smiths, not to mention their
participation together in the Woods' Movement.

Later in Kirtland we hear Joseph, Sr., telling the Pratts
that they were all relatives back in the early days. ". . . Smith
who told his sixth cousins Orson and Parley Pratt in the
1830s that their 'fathers and his all sprang from the same
man a few generations ago'" (O. Pratt 1853, p.86).

Parley Pratt's family settled in Canaan, a little village on
the eastern border of New York near Massachusetts. There
was another small town only ten miles away, just across the
Massachusetts line, called Pittsfield. From this town came
Edward Partridge, another actor in the scheme. He was
living there during the teen-age years of Parley P. Pratt. In
the late 1820s Partridge would move out to the Mentor,

Ohio, area; there he would become a very close associate to Sidney Rigdon and to the Pratts. It would be Partridge who went with Rigdon on that famous trip to Waterloo, New York, to meet Joseph Smith. This man Partridge also has to be suspicioned as a possible contributor to the birth of Mormonism as there were Partridges living in the Sharon, Vermont, and Palmyra, New York, areas. The things Partridge could have conveyed to Rigdon upon his arrival would be interesting to know. But why Rigdon chose Partridge to be the one to make that famous journey to Waterloo, New York, in December of 1830 is a mystery.

Parley P. Pratt was a "tin peddler" who traveled on the Old Indian trail that ran through the Palmyra and Manchester area. Many times during 1826 through 1829 he would certainly be one to spread the news across New York and down into Mentor, Ohio. Family history has it that Parley traveled into the Mentor area in the summer of 1826 and there he built himself a log cabin. In the summer of 1827 Parley makes another trip through New York on the old Indian Trail back to Canaan to marry a girl by the name of Thankful. By the early fall of 1827 the whole area of Palmyra and Manchester had rumors everywhere about Joseph Smith and his "gold plates." If Parley Pratt hadn't known of Joseph through family connections in Vermont, he certainly could not have traveled through the Palmyra area without having heard of "Joseph the Seer."

On 9 September 1827 Parley married in Canaan, New York. Shortly thereafter, he makes the trip back to the Mentor, Ohio area, again passing through the Palmyra area, which was now ablaze with the story of Joseph Smith and his great discovery.

If Sidney Rigdon hadn't known of Joseph before, he was sure to hear of this unimaginable account as soon as Pratt got back into town. Parley had became one of Rigdon's parishioners, and shortly thereafter was ordained as a preacher of Rigdon's faith. With Parley peddling his wares up and down the Old Indian Trail, he definitely becomes a prime suspect in the Rigdon-Smith conspiracy. His later apostleship could have been his pay back for his faithfulness in relaying the communications via Smith and Rigdon.

Rigdon was witnessed by many, including Alexander Campbell, the founder of the Disciples of Christ, who stated that Rigdon had been speaking quite enthusiastically of a new religion about to come forth, along with a new bible (and so forth), two years before the Mormon Book was written. Rigdon would have told Campbell this in 1827 or 1828, as the Book of Mormon was not published until March 1830.

In August of 1830 Rigdon sends Parley Pratt on a mission into New York where he just happens to run into one of those Smith–Rigdon–Spaulding books called the Book of Mormon. Rigdon's boy, Pratt, who had just the day before been preaching for Rigdon, quickly leafed through the "Mormon Bible" and in short order confessed his desire to be a part of this new religion. Oliver Cowdery obliged his old friend and baptized Pratt 1 September 1830, and the same evening ordained him a Mormon elder. (One of Joseph Smith's popular doctrines was to lay hands on no man suddenly.) Well you wouldn't want to leave a preacher "out in the cold," so Oliver wrapped the blanket of Mormon authority around Mr. Pratt with a "sudden laying on of hands."

One would think that having found this "glorious gospel," and now freshly anointed into its apostolic priesthood, that Pratt would be eager to relay the "unspeakable news" back to Sidney Rigdon. According to the Mormons, Sidney Rigdon would have to wait one–and–a–half months till Parley returned before he could discover what had happened to his missionary, whom he had sent over into New York.

Rigdon knew where he was sending Pratt. Pratt knew where he was going. During the time when Pratt was baptized by Oliver, there is another interesting two-to two–and–one–half months gap in Rigdon's itinerary. Rigdon was probably there at the baptism. But whether he was or not matters little, for the foundation stones were being laid.

Who ever heard of a missionary going into the mission field, so close to home, and failing to report his activities for a month–and–a–half? Then, when he does report, he shows up as a minister in a "strange new organization"; and within thirty-six hours baptizes his former overseer into the new religion. Pratt writes, "Mr. Rigdon embraced the doctrine through my instrumentality. I first presented the Book of Mormon to him. . . ." (*RLDS History*, Vol. 1, p. 145). How interesting!

Rigdon not only held in his hand Spaulding's manuscript in print, but held a book whose claims paralleled that of the Holy Bible. The first great stone of the Mormon conspiracy had been laid, with Parley Pratt having played one of the major roles.

Evidence that Pratt partook of the same anointing as did the "Mormon Seer" is well documented in the following prophecy.

Writing in 1838, apostle Parley P. Pratt said the following: "Now, Mr. Sunderland, . . . I will state as a prophesy, that there will not be an unbelieving Gentile upon this continent 50 years hence; and if they are not greatly scourged, and in a great measure overthrown, within five or ten years from this date, then the Book of Mormon will have proved itself false" (*Mormonism Unveiled–Truth Vindicated*, by Parley P. Pratt, p.15; copied from a microfilm of the original at the Mormon church historian's library by Jerald and Sandra Tanner, *The Changing World of Mormonism*, p. 420).

Some years later Parley would obtain a polygamous wife from the state of Arkansas; she would follow him to Utah. A short while later they would return to Arkansas and attempt to obtain the children from her former husband. The husband soon learned of their efforts and overtook Pratt a few miles down the road and there Parley P. Pratt was to lose his life.

CHAPTER TEN

Slicing It Up in Waterloo

❖

Sidney Rigdon was baptized into Mormonism the middle of November 1830 near his home in Mentor, Ohio. By early December Rigdon had made his way to the "side" of Joseph Smith, the Mormon prophet, out in Waterloo, New York. Smith's church was organized on 6 April 1830 some seven months before Rigdon leaves for Waterloo-Fayette, New York. Although Smith's church was holding meetings and had experienced some growth, everything appeared to be on hold until "Rigdon claimed his rightful place."

No sooner does Rigdon arrive in Waterloo, New York, to make Smith's "acquaintance," when a special revelation issues from Smith declaring, ". . . and now this calling and commandment give I unto you concerning all men, that as many as shall come before my servants Sidney Rigdon and Joseph Smith, Jr., embracing this calling and commandment shall be ordained and sent forth to preach the everlasting gospel . . ." (*RLDS D&C*, Sec 35, p. 78).

This revelation to Sidney Rigdon in December 1830 comes just three weeks after Rigdon's baptism into Mormonism. Rigdon is immediately given the highest seat of administrative authority alongside Smith. The creation of a Mormon hierarchy was initiated "pronto" upon Rigdon's arrival. Suddenly, almost as lightening from the sky, Rigdon bypasses every Mormon but the "Seer" himself and steps on "center stage" with Smith. Oliver Cowdery, Martin Harris, and David Whitmer, three men who had been chosen as the book's special witnesses, men who had burned the midnight oil, spent their money feeding, housing, and clothing Smith; and by their labor had helped bring the church to its December position, just as suddenly, notwithstanding that they were "heaven's" most favored witnesses of "Smith's plates," experienced immediate demotion upon the arrival of Rigdon. Why? How could this "stranger" have merited such a position in that short of a time?

Upon Rigdon's arrival, he and Smith would begin the task of creating a Mormon translation of the "Bible" which would later be called the Inspired Version. Rigdon, a Mormon for only a few weeks, sits down with Smith to re-write the Bible. Smith's relative and faithful scribe for the Book of Mormon, Oliver Cowdery, certainly must have understood when this "stranger" appeared and took his place.

When the first Mormon priesthood was born it was Cowdery and Smith. But later when the greater and more authoritative Melchizedek priesthood was instituted, the main heads of it were Rigdon and Smith.

But when they began work on the Bible, Rigdon, according to the *Mormon History*, had just recently been converted and certainly had not had time to be appraised of the great angelic mysteries of Smith's Kingdom. (He was one of those preachers of which "God," according to Smith, had warned him about.) Rigdon had to be one, because Smith testified that God said that, "All of them were corrupt, that everyone had gone astray, and all taught for doctrines commandments of men." Yet, Smith throws this special warning from "God" to the wind and with open arms instantaneously embraces Rigdon into the holy Mormon priesthood, placing him at his right side of authority.

This "Disciple Preacher," according to Mormon history, was a total "stranger" to Smith just a few short days before, and was preaching a gospel according to Smith's God which was "an abomination in His sight." Smith somehow sees God as having a change of mind and makes a special compromise in Rigdon's behalf, and allows Smith to immediately install

Rigdon as the one to interpret the doctrines and to assist him in re-writing the Holy Scriptures. Surely, at this moment the heavenly computers must have needed reprogramming to correct all of God's misjudgments and make amends for all that God had mistakenly told Smith.

In my visit with the present pastor of Rigdon's former Disciple Church in Mentor, Ohio, he stated that Sidney was very strong-willed and very outspoken in his beliefs, as all who knew him would vouch, but when the green horn Mormon missionaries handed him Smith's Book of Mormon, he immediately became extremely meek and offered little or no argument. He stated that Rigdon's behavior, as witnessed by his friends and congregation, was totally out of "sync" and because of this it caused several to suspicion his actions as evidence that he was a party to the whole Mormon scheme.

Let Us Summarize Rigdon's Instant Rise

According to "Mormon history" Joseph Smith and Sidney Rigdon never met until some time in December of 1830. The Mormons had been holding meetings since the middle of 1829 and had organized their church 6 April 1830. Rigdon leaves his flock (church), shirks all his spiritual responsibility, and heads to Smith's home in Waterloo in the cold of December. Rigdon, without any investigation of Smith (or Smith of Rigdon), is placed at the head of the church with Smith.

Some time between 1820 and 1830 Smith's god changed his mind, for in 1820, according to Smith, God met with him in the woods of Manchester, New York, and told him that "all the professors (preachers) were corrupt." All of them according to Smith's own words.

But before Rigdon was barely dry from his Mormon baptism, we find this god saying to this corrupt professor, "Behold, verily, verily I say unto my Servant Sidney, I have looked upon thee and thy works. I have heard thy prayers and have prepared thee for a greater work" (*Utah D&C*, Sec. 35). (Apparently this god, which manifested a changeable nature, accepts responsibility for Rigdon's corruption after all.) Anyway, Smith proceeds to say that God had prepared Rigdon for the Mormon ministry. "Thou art blessed, for thou shalt do great things. Behold thou wast sent forth even as John (the Baptist) to prepare the way before me, and before Elijah which should come, and thou knew it not" (*RLDS D&C*, Sec. 34:2). Apparently, according to the spirit that gave this revelation, "all the preachers" weren't corrupt after all, at least not Rigdon.

Well, if Rigdon was to prepare the way before "Smith," symbolized as John the Baptist who prepared the way before Jesus, then who is Smith to be likened unto? Jesus, of course, "God in the flesh." Any wonder Smith was to later say, "I am a God unto you." What Sidney Rigdon did not do was to decrease, as did John the Baptist. But under Smith's anointed revelation he was changed from "corruption to incorruption," received his crown of dominion, power, authority, and glory in the Mormon Kingdom. (Instant exaltation became a very popular Mormon doctrine.) The answer is relatively simple, Mormonism was a cake baked by Rigdon and Smith in 1826 or 1827, and the time finally came at Waterloo, New York, in December of 1830, where they sat down to slice it up.

I think it is very noteworthy that Rigdon and Smith laid out their original "battle plans" in or near the town of Waterloo. How prophetic for the two Mormon prophets! Their reign, just like Napoleon's, would come to an abrupt end within fifteen years.

Rigdon's "fore-running ministry" meant something far different than what most Mormons read into the revelation. To them it was all of Sidney's preaching on the "Western Reserve," but to Smith it was the unseen contributions of counsel, tutoring of Smith, and the Spaulding material which Rigdon had supplied months before the Book of Mormon was published. Rigdon didn't go to Waterloo to meet Smith, they had met a long time before. Rather, he went to take his pre-agreed-upon position. He went as a "stranger" (as the Mormons would have you believe) and moved in with Smith for two months. There he stayed at Smith's side through the rest of December, the month of January, and on into early February, whereupon a revelation was received in harmony with the counsel which Rigdon had been giving Smith. They were instructed to move the new headquarters to Kirtland, Ohio, Rigdon's backyard.

From this point in time Rigdon would remain second in command. He eventually would be ordained a prophet, seer, and revelator, and would occupy in this great position of power until Smith's assassination in 1844. Their conspiracy of "shared power" is evident when on 14 March 1842, Rigdon and Smith became Masons, the next day "together" advancing to the Master Mason Degree. When Joseph Smith was preparing to run for the presidency of the United States, his running mate was none other than Sidney Rigdon.

Joseph Smith knew that Rigdon's knowledge of church organization, doctrine, missionary work, tithes, propagandizing the ministry, and so forth was absolutely essential if Mormonism was to be successfully established as a church. Many of Rigdon's fundamental beliefs are distinctly laid out in the Book of Mormon. Many of these doctrines Rigdon preached while a minister in the Disciples of Christ Church. The Disciples were loudly trumpeting the restoration of the New Testament gospel, baptism by immersion, the establishment of the ancient order of things, restoring of the church, and a call to unity.

These doctrines became the early heartbeat of the message proclaimed by the Mormon missionaries. Rigdon himself was a strong advocate of the doctrine of "all things common," a doctrine so gloriously portrayed in III Nephi of the Book of Mormon. This teaching of Rigdon's was immediately instituted in the church at Kirtland under the guise of "The Order of Enoch," but was soon abandoned as many began to see it as a slick financial scheme on the part of Rigdon and Smith.

But in less than three years Smith and Rigdon would be seen herding their new converts into western Missouri, where this same doctrine was enforced. This financial scheme was called the Order of Enoch, but their new Bible home was called the Land of Zion. Thousands in just a few short years would flock to Missouri during the 1830s, as they were led to believe that soon the Land of Zion was to become as the "Garden of Eden." The city of Zion would become a place of refuge as soon as there would be an overspreading of abomination and the saints would very shortly have to flee to Zion for safety.

A conspiracy at some point always exposes itself. There are several such exposures in the Rigdon-Smith conspiracy, but none as egomaniacal as the following one. Smith inserted into the early section of his Mormon Book a prophecy of himself which covers approximately two pages. In this prophecy Smith would call himself a "Seer," but this time he would have God calling him a "Seer," and not his Palmyra neighbors. His prophecy goes on to say that he would be great like unto Moses, and that he would be called Joseph after the Book of Mormon prophet. But so that no one would misunderstand that the prophecy pertained to him, he declares that his name would be after the name of his father. (Smith was a junior.)

Now, if Smith was to be the "Great Seer," then Rigdon's position would need to be equally as important; not as flashy, but as essential, so for Rigdon his role would be prophesied as one who would be the "mouthpiece" for this "Great Seer" Joseph Smith (Book of Mormon, II Nephi 2:10-38). Sidney Rigdon being made a part of this Book of Mormon prophecy is conclusive evidence that Smith and Rigdon had long schemed their positions before the book ever rolled off the press. We can read of their scheme in the Book of Mormon, II Nephi, 2:37, "And the Lord said unto me also, I will raise up unto the fruit of thy loin: And I will make for him (Joseph Smith) a spokesman."

Regarding this Book of Mormon prophecy, Smith was able to keep silent for nearly three years after his movement began, before he reveals who this curious "spokesman" might be. No doubt Smith and Rigdon felt that after three years it was safe to reveal this man of prophecy. Therefore, by revelation on 12 October 1833, Smith identifies his "spokesman." Or rather, his god does it for him. The revelation reads: "And it is expedient in me that you, my servant Sidney, should be a 'spokesman' unto this people; yea, verily, I will ordain you unto this calling, even to be a 'spokesman' unto my servant Joseph" (*RLDS D&C*, Sec 97:3A).

The scheme of Rigdon and Smith is obviously exposed in this revelation. Sometime in 1827 Smith was chosen the "prophet" and Rigdon the "spokesman." Smith would be likened unto Moses and Rigdon likened unto Aaron; to-

gether they wrote themselves into the Mormon Scriptures.
Rigdon was ordained an elder shortly after his baptism, but
on 18 March 1833, he was ordained into the presidency of
the high priesthood, which made Rigdon equal in holding
the keys of the Kingdom with Smith. But still, he was to
receive yet another ordination; yes, to the office of "The
Spokesman." This ordination would set Rigdon and Smith
completely apart from any and all other Mormons holding
the priesthood. There is no parallel in Scripture except for
Moses and Aaron in the Old Testament. But for Smith to be
as great a prophet as Moses, he must enjoy all the privileges
that God had originally given unto Moses, and have his own
"spokesman," even though Joseph's neighbors had said that
he was quite a speaker when a teen-ager.

The dictionary says a "spokesman" is one who speaks for
another, especially one who is chosen. Well, Sidney Rigdon
was chosen all right. He was also included in the Book of
Genesis which he and Smith re-worked. Their new Bible
carried the followed prophecy of Moses and Smith, "And I
will make a spokesman for him, and his name shall be called
Aaron. And it shall be done unto thee (Smith) in the last
days also" (Inspired Version, Genesis 50:36). Smith's "interpolation" is making reference that he, the great end-time
latter day "seer," would have his "Aaron," just like Moses.
Smith's Aaron would be Rigdon. The above interpolation
into the Bible was done by Rigdon and Smith just a few
weeks after Rigdon became a Mormon.

At the dedication of the Kirtland Temple in Kirtland,
Ohio, Rigdon spoke two-and-one-half hours. On 19 June
1839, in Far West, Missouri, Rigdon's notorious "Salt Sermon," which gave birth to the Mormon doctrine of "Blood
Atonement," was that day sanctioned by the Mormon Prophet
Smith. There were many occasions when Rigdon was given
the opportunity to bring their "spokesman" prophecy into
fulfillment.

Whether Rigdon's footprints can still be found on the
dirt roads of Palmyra, New York, or Harmony, Pennsylvania,
is very doubtful; but that matters little, because the "prints"
of his scheming plans with Smith remain all too vivid between the covers of the "Scriptures of Palmyra" (The Book
of Mormon).

History verifies that in 1829 the prophecy of the "spokesman" was written as a portion of the Book of Mormon. In 1831 the same prophecy was interpolated into the Holy Bible by Rigdon and Smith. The only one who has ever been named by revelation to be the "spokesman" for the "Mormon Seer" was Sidney Rigdon.

We are faced with but two choices: (1) Joseph Smith was a true prophet, prophesying of Sidney's coming when he translated the Book of Mormon (as I once believed) and (2) Joseph knew who the "spokesman" was in 1829 or before. The actions of both Smith and Rigdon in November and December of 1830 leaves no doubt that they both understood then who the "spokesman" was.

Rigdon and Smith deceived themselves into believing that the world would accept the Book of Mormon as it had already accepted the Bible. Smith would be heralded and recognized as the "Great Seer" and Rigdon would be his "Mighty Spokesman." Rigdon and Smith planned it well, as they envisioned a rise to the pinnacle of religious power and authority as Moses and Aaron had occupied as the leaders of Old Testament Israel. Smith and Rigdon, motivated by powerful spirits of pride, dreamed of becoming the Moses and the Aaron of the "End-time House of Israel."

The "Angel of Light" designed a scheme near perfection. His founding pawns served him well. Mormonism has been a deception which rides upon the backs of both Testaments of the Bible, each used where they served the cause, and wrested when they didn't.

It was in May of 1829 when the "angel" appeared to Oliver Cowdery and Joseph in the woods of Harmony, Pennsylvania. Cowdery later wrote that the voice sounded like "Rigdon." Apparently Rigdon's role of "spokesman" was in service before the "spokesman" prophecy became Mormon scripture. If you recall, Smith had prophesied to Rigdon that he was likened as John the Baptist. In the above experience in Harmony, Pennsylvania, Smith says that the angel was John the Baptist. Rigdon's itinerary shows a large gap at this time of May 1829.

David Whitmer, one of the three original witnesses of Joseph Smith's Book of Mormon, apparently was never greatly pleased about Sidney Rigdon's climb aboard the Mormon wagon. He had this to say about Rigdon, "This matter of 'priesthood,' since the days of Sidney Rigdon, has been a stumbling-block of the L.D.S . . . This matter of two Orders of Priesthoods in the Church of Christ, and lineal priesthood of the old law being in the church, all originated in the mind of Sidney Rigdon" (David Whitmer, *Address To All Believers In Christ*, p. 64).

Today, these same spirits of deception in-dwell and affect the lives of some six million souls, and this number continues to increase at an alarming rate. The question beginning to be asked is, what is Satan's consuming end-time plan for this dark religion, of which there are over one hundred factions?

This chapter will close by allowing the will of Jeremiah Brooks to be the "Spokesman." Jeremiah Brooks, the father-in-law of Sidney Rigdon, refused to release his inheritance to his daughter, Phebe Brooks Rigdon (Rigdon's wife), as long as Rigdon was alive. His will to her reads: "Thirdly I direct my (Exc) to retain the share my daughter Phebe Rigdon for and during the full term, natural life (unless she shall survive her said Sidney Rigdon) and to pay to her annually the interest there of alone and at her decease to divide the principal equally among her children. But if the said Phebe shall survive her said husband S-R- (Sidney Rigdon) then I direct the said Exc's at the decease of Sidney Rigdon to pay over to the said Phebe the full account of her share" (Will of Jeremiah Brooks, Trumbell County, Ohio).

Usually a father-in-law likes to take some pride in his son-in-law. I do mine. But here we find that the two original leaders of Mormonism had a relationship of the poorest of terms with the fathers of their wives. Neither Smith nor Rigdon ever had any success in making Mormons out of their fathers-in-law. Jethro found great delight in his son-in-law Moses. Moses, unlike Rigdon and Smith, hearkened to the voice of his father-in-law and did all that he said (Exodus 18:24).

CHAPTER ELEVEN

The Impartation
of Spiritual Curses

❖

Oliver Cowdery was one of the three original witnesses of the Book of Mormon. He would be the only one to publicly recant his testimony as to the book's validity. This denial was only the beginning of his fight for spiritual freedom from the spirits he had become subject to during his ten years as a Mormon. The years he spent with Smith would enslave him to many powerful occult spirits. Cowdery in 1838 may have physically departed Mormonism, but those deceiving spirits he partook of while in that religion would continue to battle him for the devotion of his mind and soul as long as he lived.

Cowdery had been so deeply affected by their lying presence that in his mind he could not grasp the simple truth of the plain words that Jesus would later speak to him in 1839. Shortly after leaving Mormonism Cowdery writes of that experience with the Lord:

> The Redeemer instructed me plainly: He [Joseph Smith] hath given revelations from his own heart and from a defiled conscience as coming from my mouth and hath corrupted the Covenant and altered words which I had spoken. He hath brought in high priests, apostles and other officers, which in these days the Written Word suffices . . . He walketh in the vain imaginations of his

113

heart, and My Spirit is Holy and does not dwell in an unholy Temple, nor are angels sent to reveal the great work of God to hypocrites. (Oliver Cowdery's Defense)

According to Oliver the Lord stood before him and told him the above, yet Cowdery experienced great difficulty in grasping the full content of what Jesus was saying to him. This blockage in the mind of Cowdery by these occult powers is born out in a previous paragraph in the same defense, where he writes, ". . . but I fear I may have been deceived, and especially so fear since knowing that Satan led his mind astray." Cowdery says, "I fear I may have been deceived." He wasn't sure that he had been deceived, even after Jesus had distinctly revealed to him that he had been deceived. This is a good illustration of the clever working of deceiving spirits operating in the mind of a man. These spirits prevented him from having a full comprehension of the truth which would have set him free. In light of the fact that Jesus clearly told Oliver that Smith walked in the imaginations of his own heart, that He did not lead him, that his revelations came from a defiled conscience, and that God does not send angels to hypocrites, Cowdery still could not see far enough through the maze of the spiritual darkness, which possessed him, to be able to recognize how great his need was for further deliverance.

Many were the religious spirits that had imbedded themselves into his personality and were warring against his mind as he was attempting to walk toward the light that would set him free. The "spirits" he partook of in those few weeks with Joseph in writing the Book of Mormon still held him captive. The supernatural visitation he had encountered at Smith's side remained very real to him. The hypnotic control which he was suffering under was so impressionable upon his mind that the words of Jesus alone were not enough to restore to him a sound mind.

Those who have sought to become free from such deceiving influences after allowing them to spread a great nest in their souls, as did Cowdery, know the reality of the battle that rages before freedom is possible. According to Oliver the Lord said, "Neither have I sent angels." Had Oliver been able to drink deeply of these words of Jesus he would have received the strength and the wisdom to have completely broken any remaining power the deceiving spirits held in his mind.

I experienced this same type of control as I was attempting to leave Mormonism. The Book of Mormon was my last Mormon object which remained deeply imbedded into my emotions. I can understand some of the battle and struggle which Cowdery encountered. It was very difficult to break the enchanting spell of that book and accept the fact that it was a lie. These spirits of sentimentality bond the soul of an individual to a deception to such an excessive degree that one's mind is unable to entertain the thought that what they believe may be a lie. The Bible says, "The prophets prophesy falsely . . . and my people love to have it so . . ." (Jeremiah 5:31). These spirits impart a love for such false things. This love can become so dear and deep that Jesus himself cannot set the person free because they would not want His interference in the first place.

The stronger one's beliefs are in an "occult religion," the deeper the deception penetrates into the soul of the believer. In such a religion there can be no deception apart from deceiving spirits. The extent of the deception reveals how far the spirit has stretched his wings of occupation within the believer. These spirits develop in the individual's very warm and deep emotional "soul ties" which can totally control the rationality of the person. This type of control is very evident in the lives of most Mormons, as their minds are usually closed to any outside spiritual teaching. Oliver Cowdery may have taken many of these "soul ties" with him to the grave. The roots of such emotions sometimes are long in dying, and will never die if the individual continues to desire some fellowship with the author of those feelings.

Whether Cowdery perceived everything that Smith had in his magic arsenal we do not know. We do know that Joseph Smith at times deceived his family, his friends, and anyone who would listen to his word. Oliver later marveled over this mysterious power Smith held over him, as well as the strangeness of the situation while they were working on the Book of Mormon. Cowdery in his own confession stated that he had believed that Smith was a prophet, and that he believed in his "seer stone." This belief is evident in that Cowdery kept one of Smith's seer stones in his possession until his death. Cowdery's attachment and belief in this occult object, which demons had operated though, most definitely gave those spirits of deception a legal right to remain with him. These spirits would have clouded his mind, and would have never ceased in their efforts to persuade him of how wrong he was, and that he should go back to where he belongs, and sing once again the old songs of Zion.

When an individual, innocent or otherwise, participates in rituals where fallen angels are called up (conjured), such as Joseph did for the three witnesses to the Book of Mormon, there is always a price exacted by the satanic spirit which performs this work. When these spirits perform such labors for the sorcerer the spirits are aware that the participants are fair game for habitation.

The kind of spirits that would have entered the three witnesses of the Book of Mormon, Oliver Cowdery, Martin Harris, and David Whitmer, that day would have been spirits of false visions, clairvoyance, telepathy, false prophecy, seducing spirits, and spirits of delusions. The spirits of religious deception are extremely powerful and often vindictive; they will work night and day upon the individual to keep them in that state of deception. Smith's three witnesses to the Book of Mormon were very naive in spiritual matters, or they would not have yielded themselves into the hands of a man who had been steeped in the occult for years. Their very eyes had witnessed his occult "crystal gazing" methods. Each had been given revelations through the "stone." When we lay aside all scriptural guard as did these men, we have invited deception to come in.

The moment a preacher proclaims that his doctrines and his church are the only correct ones, he has entered into "witchcraft." For what follows then is the attempt to persuade and manipulate the minds of others to believe as he does. When we ask someone then to pray to God over a matter of a "true church" or a "true book," it is to ask them to enter into the same deception. No religion which has the true Spirit of Jesus Christ will ever lead someone down a path which encourages them to bypass the scripture which says, "To prove all things and hold fast to that which is good" (I Thessalonians 5:21).

Mormons since the days of Smith have encouraged people to pray to God for a supernatural witness of the Book of Mormon, thus encouraging people to bypass all scriptural counsel laid out in the Word of God, which admonishes all men not to entertain doctrines and deeds that are in any way contrary to its Divine Truth. This deceptive counsel which directs an individual to pray to God for a witness of the truth of the Book of Mormon is taken from the book itself. The number of supernatural manifestations which have been experienced by the unwary seeker is astounding. These supernatural encounters in the spirit world operate upon a person in much the same way as a hook does in the mouth of a fish. Once an individual is hooked by such a manifestation he then can be maneuvered in what ever direction the spirit so desires. This "witchcraft" has resulted in tens of thousands of Mormon converts receiving visitations from the same deceiving spirits that wrecked spiritual havoc in the lives of Cowdery, Whitmer, and Harris.

The very "Narrow Way" put forth in the New Testament by Jesus and preached by His disciples is the faith every person must walk in, or else they will become fair game to be sacrificed upon the altar of deception. We are to preach Jesus and Him crucified, not ourselves, not some prophet, not some special revelation produced by "crystal gazers," and not some church and its organization. The moment we accept witchcraft teaching such as Mormonism we have accepted the occult, and openly invite the curses of demonic sophistry, religious pride, and deception to invade our soul.

Some of the spirits which have descended through the generations of Mormonism are: special visitations, dreams, hearing voices, dramatic manifestations regarding the Book of Mormon, as well as receiving visits from dead relatives. These experiences often provide a subjective witness, which informs the recipients that their prophets are of God and their church is the only true one. The results of these experiences have produced a severe crystallization of attitudes, as well as a very extreme belief of possessing unique favoritism with God. Believing themselves to be divine favorites is evidence that they have partaken of very powerful spirits of pride and self righteousness. I have listened to many such testimonies over the years.

I watched a school teacher weep as she testified of David O. McKay (then the president of the Utah Mormon Church) as being a true prophet of God. Little did she know that God would have led her out of Mormonism in His time and brought her upon a sound basis of His Word. Rather, her desire was to obtain a supernatural manifestation that McKay was God's anointed. She was asked to begin praying that God would give her a special spiritual witness of McKay. She received a very vivid experience but never tested the spirit that came. She excitedly accepted the aberration as evidence that the Lord had spoken to her. Now not only does she have in her possession a supernatural experience but also has a supernatural spirit. She, by this spirit's power, can weep and boldly testify very convincingly to the innocent and unwary of the divine authority of Mormonism. She has gotten herself so far out into deception that she had become a pawn of that "spirit." Now, she could be told most anything by this spirit, or by Mormon leaders, and believe it without question.

Carol Hanson, a former Mormon Handmaiden, shares in her book *The RLDS Church: Christian?* the reality of these spirits' deceiving power and the spiritual games that they played for a time in their lives. She writes:

> Our spiritual experiences were the compelling force that drove us to continue the "Lord's Mission." These experiences ranged from visions and dreams, to audible voices, "miracles," and prophetic utterances. In one vision, I was shown the sealed portion of the Book of Mormon and was told that our group would receive this record when we met certain conditions. When things we were told failed to occur, we were always reassured by a "still small voice" which said, "Don't give up, you have been brought thus far as a trial of your faith." After seven years of unfulfilled dreams, failed prophecies, and witnessing the devastating effect my involvement was having on my family, I was forced to admit that it was not the Lord, but deceiving spirits I had been listening to. (Carol M. Hansen, *The RLDS Church: Christian?*, p. 7-8)

There are thousands of like testimonies of "spirit visitations" among the Latter Day Saints (LDS). Some of these visits have to do with what is called the "sealed portion of the Book of Mormon," or the plates which Joseph Smith said he could not translate because they were "sealed" and the time would come when they could be revealed. The individual unto whom God would choose to bring this "great revelation" to light would be called "mighty and strong;" he would be a prophet, seer, and revelator just as Joseph Smith had claimed to be. (Although I believe Joseph had planned the role for himself.)

I have personally met several Mormons who have laid claim to this "majestic" calling, all of whom were visited by some "angel." All of these individuals were granted the privy of knowing that they were the "Mighty and Strong One." That they were the special chosen instrument and personally handpicked by God to finally reveal this last grand hidden mystery of Moroni's God. This satanic Moroni could very well fulfill this long awaited dream of the Mormons and give them the desire of their hearts!

One of these persons was visited by this spirit Moroni, who told him that God chose him to be the "Mighty and Strong One." He was at the time living in Southern California and attending the same congregation as I. There were several occasions when we discussed the Book of Mormon, and on one of these he took me in his confidence to share how the angel Moroni had appeared to him with the plates in hand for him to view, and had informed him that he was called to translate these "sealed records" by the Urim and Thummim. The gravity of his story was quite convincing as it was accompanied with tears and much sincerity. I was deeply affected by his testimony for a long time, and was yet a Mormon myself; therefore I was very impressed that this most famous angel, Moroni, had so highly favored him as to personally visit him at his home.

There was another Latter Day Saint elder who told me of a particular angel who claimed to be "Joseph Smith" appearing to a group of people in India, telling them that he was a true prophet with the keys of the priesthood of Heaven for this last dispensation of time. He told them that he would send a Mormon elder to them with the gospel and ordain them into this true priesthood of God. This Mormon elder shared with me his trip to India and the ordaining of these men into his segment of Mormonism. This man had several spiritual experiences which made him to know that God had called him to be the one "Mighty and Strong." He had been told by this spirit calling himself Joseph Smith that he was to stand in Smiths' stead as God's prophet, seer, and revelator, holding the keys of God's end-time priesthood authority upon the earth. This man and I visited together for over three hours one afternoon in 1974. He had come with a special revelation for me, counseling me to become a part of his ministry. I told this man that he was the third or fourth "prophet" who had come to me bearing a similar message, and that personally I did not believe that any of these revelations had come from the Lord Jesus Christ, and had my doubts that Joseph Smith was even in heaven. This man also believed that he was the one to translate the "sealed" plates of Moroni.

In 1972, just prior to our moving to the "Land of Zion," Independence, Missouri, my wife and I were given a very powerful prophecy in our home one evening. This supposed word of the Lord was given by a Mormon prophetess from the Los Angeles, California, area. This prophecy stated that my wife and I were to return to Missouri and complete the work of Joseph and Emma Smith. This prophecy would be the first of several such "divine instructions" intimating that my calling was to at least parallel that of Joseph Smith.

Three years later, one of the most respected prophetesses among the "Mothers of Israel" was to share the following with me which she had received through the "spirit:"

> To My Servant Barney—beloved of the Lord—called and ordained and set apart for a high and Holy calling— Filled with the spirit of Elias, the restorer of all things to their proper order as they are appointed by the Father in Heaven. . . . Many people have hated you and believed you not as under My power and direction, you have exposed the evil and corruption that exists and they have refused to harken even as they refused to harken unto

Me, Your Master, when I walked amongst them and exposed the evils and hypocrisy of that day.

Also many have loved you . . . and are looking to you as a Servant in the Hand of God to bring deliverance from the bondage that has been so hard to bear. . . .

My blueprint is ready and available for the asking and I am calling to you even as I called unto Nephi to receive instruction from My Hand . . . You are a descendant of Lehi, even of little Joseph and I have raised you up for this hour, even as I promised to little Joseph when his father Lehi blessed him and I will not fail you. My spirit is upon you and shall come upon you even in greater power and you shall be made equal to the task whereunto I have called you.

. . . Nephi did not build the ship after the manner of men and neither shall you build My Church after the manner of men for this is the Church of the Living God, endowed with faith in all its power and splendor . . . that My Kingdom even Zion might come upon the face of the earth. . . . Thou art My Chosen Instrument to do this work for Me. . . . (This prophecy was dated 13 February 1975.)

I was still very deep into Mormonism at this time, and due to certain prevailing circumstance which were going on, this "revelation" from Satan through one of his special handmaidens attempted to lure me into a high level of deception. God in His mercy enabled me to ascertain the source from which this "revelation" came. This is but one example of how the spirits of false prophecy continues to deceive and manipulate the lives of Mormon believers. The danger of it all is that so many Mormons deeply yearn in their hearts to receive from the "Lord" such a prophetic word.

The following gives a graphic picture of how these spirits among the Mormons go about their works of deception. This particular segment of Mormonism branched off the Utah Mormons of Salt Lake. I shall quote part of an article titled "The Coming Forth of the Sealed Portion of the Book of Mormon." On 25 January 1981, after David had left the group led by John Bryant (Church of Christ, Patriarchal) along with many others, the Lord commanded him to establish a version of the Church of the Firstborn bearing the name Sons Ahman Israel. This covenant and organization was sealed by immersion at Saratoga Hot Springs, Utah, at dawn the following day, it being exactly one hundred-forty-five years since Joseph Smith's attended restoration (the third restoration) of the patriarchal Church of the Firstborn at Nauvoo, Illinois.

> Emergence of a unique set of scriptures for this church began twenty-three days later with the appearance of the angels Shulem and Moroni to a sister called Hava Pratt who was then living at Fairhaven, Nevada. Beginning on 16 February 1981 the angels began to dictate to her what was later to be called the Writings of Moroni, representing a portion of the Nephite writings not found in the unsealed portion of the Book of Mormon. (Restoration, Steven Shields Pub., Vol. 7, No 4., p. 32)

After hearing so many bizarre testimonies of the spirit Moroni's continued appearances among the Mormons, I have no doubt that David Whitmer, Oliver Cowdery, and Martin Harris, the three special witnesses to the Book of Mormon, had some kind of encounter with this same spirit of Moroni. I am satisfied that they saw what they believed at the time to be an "angel" with a set of plates in his hands. So powerful was the effect upon David Whitmer that he never denied what he saw, although he and Joseph Smith became enemies later on. Whitmer was also deceived in 1830 by a young lady with a "green enchanted stone," and again by Hyrum Paige and his "stone" a short time later, as well as in 1836 with a young woman in Kirtland, Ohio, who had a "black stone." Whitmer definitely had an attraction to "seer stones," and possessed a weakness as well in being deceived by them.

Joseph Smith by the year 1829 understood the workings of the occult very well. He had been tutored several years by Luman Walters, a man well schooled in the arts of the occult. Smith's experience had by now covered a period of ten to fifteen years. He received his first "stone" in 1819 and

in 1822 he obtained his "Chase Stone," and instantly claimed
that it gave off revelations. From that date on Joseph had six
years to develop in his "aberrative priesthood." That Joseph
Smith had the gift of conjuring up spirits and receiving the
ministry of familiar spirits is well documented among his
neighbors, in his writings, and amongst the early Mormons,
including his own mother. Smith was singled out by the rank
of demon spirits which were assigned to do the work of
seduction and deception in the area of religion. These spirits
work according to the faith and the occult understanding of
the medium priest (warlock) through whom they operate.
These demons can easily seduce, hypnotize, present visions,
and so forth to any seeker within the scope of their deceptive purposes. This is one reason why the Scriptures warn
the believer not to be unequally yoked with an unbeliever (II
Corinthians 6:14).

David Whitmer, Oliver Cowdery, and Martin Harris,
Smith's three special witnesses, were not followers of Christ,
but of Smith; and in seeking after a testimony of a scheme
which the devil was fostering, they became easy prey for
deception. An "angel of light" bearing the name of Moroni
appears. The "angel" was seen in a trance-like vision standing in the air holding the plates. This occurred with Smith
at their side! It took a little while for Harris as he was a little
suspicious of Smith and could not enter into his trance with
the others around. This is evidence that it was a demonic
illusion because all three did not see it at the same time.
Martin and Joseph moved off a piece and there the vision
fell upon him. Not one of the three witnesses ever challenged or tested the spirit that day. The Bible says to try the
spirits and see if they be of God (I John 4:1). They didn't,
and all three would put their names to a document which
remains to this day, but not without a price.

Martin paid his price early on as well as later. The Re-
stored Gospel of Joseph Smith never restored Martin's soul.
Martin's mental problems and angel chasing just got worse.
Martin, who received such an outstanding manifestation at
the hand of Moroni, in a very short time was to embrace the
Shakers and Prophetess Lee where a new set of plates would

be found which, according to Harris, were just as "divine" as Smith's ever were. He would also lose his wife as she was unwilling to follow him in the illusion of Mormonism.

David and Oliver, in a few short years, had to flee from Missouri with their families under a death order from Joseph Smith (losing all their property which Smith confiscated). David and Oliver knew that Joseph Smith's Danite Avenging Angels were hot on their trail to fulfill this word of the Lord from Smith's own mouth. In only eight short years in a gospel where the law was supposed to be love, they found themselves having to run for their lives from their once-beloved prophet. Joseph Smith had his followers believing that when he spoke, it was as if it was from God's own mouth. His word had become "the way, the truth, and the life" and was not to be countered if you were to remain a saint in good standing.

It is interesting to note that soon after Joseph began to "cleanse" his house (the church) of the "dissenters" such as Cowdery, Whitmer, and etc., that he and thousands of his followers would be chased out of Missouri under a like extermination order from the governor of Missouri.

When one yields themselves (as did the Book of Mormon witnesses) into the hands of a man highly anointed with familiar spirits, they will receive spiritual bondages, deceptions, and anointings that could last for a life time.

A few years ago I spent several weeks working with a man who had been deeply involved into the occult. The powers he received from these spirits would in many respects rival Joseph Smith's occult powers. The difference between this man and Smith was that Joseph was more channeled by the high ruling spirits for a specific work that Satan desired done, while this other man was content to remain in the realm of local churches, and amidst friends and family whereby he could leave his occult heritage. I never met anyone, including pastors, who did not believe that this man possessed a great gift of the Holy Spirit. He only needed to meditate upon you for a few seconds, and he could see you in a vision and what you were doing. If you had troubled areas in your body he could see and describe them. He could observe the demons as they moved amidst the TV programs performing their deceptions and imparting their spirits to the viewers. Daily the demons would step off the screen and commune with him in his living room. He could "astral project" anywhere he chose to go, as the demons assisted him. In one moment he could be in Houston and the next he could be spying on a business partner in Kansas City. He was given powers of clairvoyancy, telepathy, possession of a third eye, and many other powerful spirits. We witnessed scores of spirits leave him as he desired to be free.

Joseph Smith in like manner passed on through the "Laying on of Hands" the great company of spirits that swarmed about him and anointed him. Since these "religious spirits" operate with great similarity to the Holy Spirit seldom are they ever detected. By and large most Mormons desire to receive this ministry, believing that it is from Heaven.

The following testimonies are more evidence of the working of deceiving spirits. These testimonies are of a former "New Ager," who in recent years accepted Christ as his Savior. His involvement into crystal-gazing carries a close similarity to the methods and experiences of Joseph Smith.

"Here's How It Began—'With a Hunk of Rock'"

Vicki had received a small but perfect quartz crystal from an American Indian medicine man, one of his "power objects." One day when doing New Age meditation she was instructed by her "spirit guides" to give me the crystal and to ask me to meditate with it. This was bizarre. The idea of meditating with a hunk of rock sounded patently ridiculous. After laughing about the idea for a couple of days, I decided to give it a shot. It couldn't hurt, could it? Only minutes after focusing on the crystal in a state of trance-like meditation, my consciousness was catapulted into electrifying domains of extra-natural light the likes of which I had never before perceived. The upper part of my head felt like it wasn't there, like it had become invisible, as my awareness raced upwards at the speed of light. This was my "crystal initiation" into an entirely different supernatural realm. Wow! Was this "crystal power" or what? For the rest of the week my crystal-aided meditations brought vivid visions of strange high-tech machines and contraptions all using crystals in different ways. It was like stepping into a science fiction novel about technologies on an alien planet. I also saw visions of high-crystal Tech holistic health clinics with lasers, holography, color beams, glowing liquids, and more in this mind boggling sci-fi film.

Riding High

Several close friends remarked on a distinct change in my demeanor. Somehow, they said, I was more charged and out going. I felt blissful, as if I had found an entirely new part of myself. Sadly, though, in reality I blindly had entered an entirely different realm of Satan's high-tech, dazzling deceptions. Sure all of this was a blast and I was riding a high like I had never known, but later there would be a very dear price to pay for all this occult adventurism. A dear price indeed. (Randall N. Baer, *Inside the New Age Nightmare*, p. 25)

A Book Materialized

A crystal power book materialized from "Heavenly Places," a modern day Book of Mormon. Approximately three months after moving to the northern New Mexico area, my "spirit guides" gave me instructions to write a book on the subject of crystals. It was only a year or so since my very first crystal experiences, and I had no idea how I could accomplish such a task. This was back in 1982-1983 when there were only a few meager and obscure crystal books on the market. It was just a year or two before the massive crystal craze would start to sweep the New Age like a raging wildfire.

Spirit Guides

The spirit guides told me to take twelve quartz crystals and lay them out in a circle, to tape another one to the occult "third eye" and to suspend a large pyramid overhead. I was to sit in the very center of the crystals with my head underneath the pyramid. This was supposed to create a "crystal energy field" having amplified "higher vibrations" for receiving channeled thoughts from the spirit guides.

> To my amazement, as I would enter a kind of semi-conscious trance, discernible thoughts, inspirations, and pictures would appear in my mind. All this was not my own doing—the spirit guides were transmitting their thoughts and influences to me. My job, effectively, was to take notes and then shape up the material into book form.

> Over a period of three months I would take my position in the crystal circle for ten to twelve hours per day and receive and transcribe this information. With some library research on the history of occult crystal use plus orthodox science's uses of man-made crystals in various technologies (like computers and lasers), the manuscript was complete. (Ibid, pp. 35-36)

Master Stone

> Shortly thereafter I went to a psychic fair in Dallas. Amid all the usual psychic readers I came upon a man calling himself "Saint. . . ." . . . .Saint loaned me his "master stone" to help me activate my consciousness onto a higher "Light-frequency." It was a strange looking, blackish, oval-shaped stone with thousands of tiny spines sticking out all around it . . . I carried this stone "power object" throughout the next few dramatic months. (Ibid, pp. 26-27)

If Joseph Smith were alive today, he would be at the forefront of the New Age movement. The spirit which Satan is releasing at this hour is unfolding natural knowledge, as well as the secret powers of the occult in unimaginable proportions. Smith's "crystal gazing" definitely marked him a prophet possessing all the characteristics of a New Ager. It would only take another visitation from Moroni with a special revelation from the "sealed portion of the Book of Mormon" to easily sweep thousands, if not millions, of Mormons into a special role for them to play in the end-time New Age deception.

CHAPTER TWELVE

Seducing
of a Neighbor

❖

Martin Harris was a fairly well–to–do farmer in the township of Palmyra, New York. In the year 1813, Harris inherited his father's farm of 121 acres. A year or so later another 29 acres would be added bringing the total size of his farm to 150 acres. Martin's most notable claim to fame came when he was selected to be one of the three witnesses to the Book of Mormon. Martin Harris was never given a leadership position in the Mormon hierarchy, although Smith did pacify him with a seat on the high council in Kirtland, Ohio, and for a while did permit him to travel with the Mormon elite, but for reasons not given he was directed by Joseph to travel alone in his missionary efforts (*RLDS Church History*, V.I., p.35). For nearly seven years Harris appeared content with the popular role Smith had given him. But in 1837 he, along with many others, began to follow after the revelations of a prophetess seer there in Kirtland, Ohio. His adamancy over this young seeress and her "black stone" was more than Smith could take. He refused to submit to Smith's demands and was excommunicated.

One Kirtland resident inferred, concerning Harris's mind, that it was "always unbalanced on the subject of Mormonism, had become so demented that he thought himself bigger than Smith, or even Christ" (C.G. Crary, *Pioneer and*

Personal Reminiscences, p. 41). Perhaps from this statement alone one can see how easily Harris could have been manipulated and mesmerized by Smith. The seduction of Martin Harris by the Mormon prophet was a spiritual epitaph which would long remain in the minds of the inhabitants of Palmyra, New York.

His former wife, Lucy Harris, wrote in 1833 concerning her onetime man:

> Martin was once industrious, attentive to his domestic concerns, . . . He is naturally quick in his temper, and in his mad-fits frequently abuses all who may dare to oppose him in his wishes. However strange it may seem, I have been a great sufferer by his unreasonable conduct. At different times while I lived with him, he has whipped, kicked and turned me out of the house. About a year previous to the report being raised that Smith had found gold plates, he became very intimate with the Smith family, and said he believed Joseph could see in his stone anything he wished. (Charles A. Shook, *The True Origin of Mormonism*, p. 46)

I would like to interject at this point that the period of time of which she is speaking is the year 1826. The Mormon history will lead you to believe that Harris and Smith were strangers until the fall of 1827, when Harris advanced Smith fifty dollars to make a trip to Pennsylvania. The Smiths had settled in Palmyra in 1815-1816, just a mile or so from the Harris farm. The truth is, Harris had known the Smiths for nearly ten years before he would fall into the snare of Smith's spell.

Lucy Harris continues:

> After this he apparently became very sanguine in his belief, and frequently said he would have no one in his house that did not believe in Mormonism; and because I would not give credit to the report he made about the gold plates, he became more austere towards me. . . . Whether the Mormon religion be true or false, I leave the world to judge, for its effects upon Martin Harris have been to make him more cross, turbulent and abusive to me. His whole object was to make money by it. . . . It is vain for the Mormons to deny these facts; for

they are all well known to most of his former neighbors. The man has now become an object of pity; he has spent most of his property, and lost the confidence of his former friends. (Ibid, p. 46-47)

The Palmyra facts are that Harris would have known the Smiths some ten or twelve years before, becoming infatuated by the schemes of the young spiritist seer. Martin had one great weakness of which many of his neighbors were aware, that being his love for the spectacular. Smith's sensitive perception had long appraised Harris as possessing this childlike vulnerability. Although Harris may not have been able to compete with Smith's cunning, he was quoted by his sister-in-law, Abigail Harris, as telling his wife Lucy, "What if it is a lie; if you will let me alone I will make money out of it" (Ibid, p. 48).

In the *Palmyra Courier* dated 24 May 1872, we read: Martin Harris married his own cousin, Dolly (Lucy) Harris; a union which, though contrary to laws and customs, proved to be a pleasant one for both until Martin became estranged by the Mormon delusions. . . . But Martin became infatuated with the idea of a new church as described by Joe, and the promise of being an apostle, led him on, contrary to the advice of his friends and the pleading of his wife who denounced the whole affair as a piece of "ridiculous nonsense".

Martin had gotten so excited over the promises which Smith had made, as well as believing that so much glory was waiting just over the hill, that he agreed in 1828 to underwrite the publishing cost of the Book of Mormon. This agreement was not only going to cost Harris his farm, but it would also prove to cost him his young wife.

When June of 1829 rolled around and it was time to print the Book of Mormon, Harris must have been a little short on cash. Because we find Smith having to turn to his seer stone for special financial counsel. Up to now, Smith's personal "Urim and Thummim" had only dealt with some fortune telling and communing with treasure spirits. But now a real life problem is presented to the god of his stone. Smith with his seer stone was about to step into the arena where only true prophets can produce. He is now faced with a fully legitimate opportunity to validate his claims to prophethood.

Smith buries his face into his hat and in the surrounding darkness peers at the "stone." The "stone" glows in the darkness and from its light comes the revelation, "Send Oliver Cowdery and Hiram Paige to Toronto, Canada; there they will find a man anxious to purchase the copyright of the Book of Mormon" (Attested to by both David Whitmer, *Address to All Believers*, p. 31, and Oliver Cowdery, *Defense*).

Here we see Smith claiming to be God's great endtime prophet. He has just completed the translation of an ancient record which he purports that God himself was personally overseeing. According to Smith, angels had guarded its hiding for 1,400 years, and had just directed its resurrection; but now when the time has arrived for the book to be published the angels cannot be found.

Why send two men to Toronto, Canada? This city was some two hundred miles from Palmyra. How shamefully ridiculous this revelation proved to be. Who could guess the number of times the "stone" had failed Joseph when he sought gold in the hills of New York and Pennsylvania. Perhaps all the failures may have been the reason why he was willing to stage the find at Cumorah. This revelation instructing the copyright to be sold, leaves one with a definite view that the Book of Mormon was intended as a Book for MORe MONey.

Cowdery and Paige returned from Toronto empty-handed. The man did not materialize! The revelation from the rising Mormon seer was false. Cowdery wrote, "We did not find him and had to return surprised and disappointed. I well remember how hard I strove to drive away the foreboding which seized me, that the First Elder (Smith) had made fools of us, where we thought in simplicity of our hearts that we were divinely commanded" (Oliver Cowdery, *Defense*).

This was Mormonism's first major "wild goose chase," a Canadian one at that. This stone found in Willard Chase's well definitely had the curse of "chase" upon it. Maybe as well also the "chase"tisement of God.

Joseph, burned by one revelation, turns to his stone

again. This time he produces a revelation with more practicality, and apparently within the geographical working ranges of his spirit guides. The revelation is directed toward Martin Harris, the scribe of the "lost" 116 pages, of which his wife Lucy was believed to have been the destroying angel. In this revelation Smith turns toward Harris with a fury, riding upon him with a spirit of guilt and condemnation, as well as carrying his sins before the world, pronouncing the worst of curses upon him if he does not obey his demands, and pay for the book to be printed.

The revelation reads,

> I command you to repent, repent, lest I smite you by the rod of my mouth, and by my wrath, and by my anger, and your sufferings be sore. How sore you know not. How exquisite you know not! Yea, how hard to bear you know not! . . . and I command thee that thou shalt not covet thine own property, but impart it freely to the printing of the Book of Mormon, . . . And Misery thou shalt receive if thou shalt slight these counsels, yea even the destruction of thyself and property. . . . Pay the printer's debt!! Release thyself from bondage! (*Book of Commandments*, Chapter XVI, p. 31-32)

Martin had on one known occasion given Smith fifty dollars in his time of need. In February of 1828, he had traveled to New York City at his own expense to seek professional proof that Joseph's work was of divine origin. He had spent many weeks at his own expense helping Smith with the writing of the book in Pennsylvania. This kindness and generosity was all water under the bridge. Now Smith is desperate, and Harris is the only believer within his control who possesses sufficient means to pay for the printing of the book. But it is obvious that it makes no difference to Smith that Harris will have to sell his only means of livelihood to pay for the Book of Mormon. As a matter of fact, he commands it in the revelation. Thus Smith uses this most forceful abuse of a supposed word of God to bring Harris to a willing obeisance.

A revelation containing curses of this magnitude spoken through the mouth of an accomplished warlock such as Smith could cause serious consequences to the person who refuses to comply. It is no doubt that the "spirits" bore their witness when Harris meditated upon the revelation. Disobedience to the word carried the penalty of great suffering, and even death. Joseph's "god" was manifesting a color which would be unique to Mormonism. Harris had to respond immediately or else curses of the greatest magnitude were going to descend upon the "sinner man." This revelation given to Martin Harris very vividly portrays the character of the "strange fire" which would forge the Mormon religion. One can see in the spirit of Smith a dark activity of coercive control, where vengeance and fear were the tools of his authority.

Smith became a feared man from the outset, this being mainly due to his ability and knowledge to release his spirit guides to bring to pass the curses he had spoken. Smith would at times give lip service to the wholesome principles of the gospel as taught by Jesus, which served only as a vehicle, used to carry out his own deceit.

But he would become the great Mormon seer where his words would become the law to all who followed him. Harris definitely partook of many of these same spirits which worked in the mind of Smith. A short time later, Harris himself was to prophesy that the little town of Palmyra would be destroyed in 1836, and by 1838 the Mormon Church would be so large that the United States would no longer need a president.

In response to the revelation, Harris quickly sold his farm and paid the printer some three thousand dollars for printing the Book of Mormon. The curses were stayed!

Smith's most sacred golden plates, which no one actually ever saw or physically ever held in their hands, carried (according to Smith) a penalty of instant death. Smith made sure no one ever learned the truth of his scheme. This spell of fear was to fall upon his friends, his entire family, including his own wife. Whether he had performed enough ritualistic sacrifices in order to release sufficient demonic power to accomplish his threat no one ever learned. But many would later learn that there were forces operating at his side which few desired to tangle.

The Satanist Anton LaVey speaks concerning a curse, "If your curse provokes their actual annihilation, rejoice that you have been instrumental in ridding the world of a pest" (Anton Szandor LaVey, *The Satanic Bible*, 1969).

Later on Martin Harris would join a faction in Kirtland, Ohio, which opposed Smith, and it rallied around a young girl who claimed to be a seeress by virtue of a "black stone" in which she read the future. David Whitmer, Martin Harris, and Oliver Cowdery . . . pledged her their loyalty, and F.G. Williams, formerly Joseph's First Counselor, became her scribe. Patterning herself after the Shakers, the new prophetess would dance herself into a state of exhaustion before her followers, fall upon the floor, and burst forth with revelations. (Fawn M. Brodie, *No Man Knows My History*, p. 205) Harris was excommunicated over believing in the young lady's revelations.

Smith had become very intolerant to any who would offer a threat to his prophetic office. Smith, extremely jealous and fearful of any competition, always cleared the church of any new rival prophets. In Smith's mind lurked a sadistic possessiveness; that if anyone was going to seduce his sheep he would be the one to do the seducing.

Martin Harris later joined the Shakers, and the prophetess Anna Lee declared that their plates were as divine as Smiths. In the 1850s Martin Harris joined the Mormons in Utah and lived the remainder of his days in the salt lands.

CHAPTER THIRTEEN

Hunting Treasures in the City of Witches

❖

In 1836 Joseph got wind of possible treasures hidden in Salem, Massachusetts; the account of this treasure hunt is recorded in Mormon history books. This Salem trip is one of the great embarrassing incidents in Mormon history. The following is the information which Smith received relative to a large treasure, which was supposedly buried in the basement of a certain house in Salem, Massachusetts (*The Return*, Vol. 1, p. 105).

> A brother in the church, by the name of Burgess, had come to Kirtland and stated that a large amount of money had been secreted in a cellar of a certain house in Salem, Massachusetts, which had belonged to a widow, and he thought he was the only person now living who had knowledge of it, or to the location of the house. We saw the brother Burgess, but Don Carlos Smith [prophet's brother] told us with regard to the hidden treasure. His statement was credited by the brethren, and steps where taken to try and secure the treasure, of which we will speak more fully in another place. (*The Return*, Vol. 1, p. 105)

> We soon learned that four of the leading men of the Mormon church had been to Salem, Massachusetts, in search of the hidden treasure spoken of by Brother Bur-

gess, viz; Joseph Smith, Hyrum Smith, Sidney Rigdon, and Oliver Cowdery. They left home on the 25th of July, 1836, and returned in September. (Ibid., p. 106)

Joseph Smith's *History* tells of this trip:

On Monday afternoon, July 25th, in company with Sidney Rigdon, Brother Hyrum Smith, and Oliver Cowdery, I left Kirtland, . . .

From New York we continued our journey to Providence, on board a steamer; from thence to Boston, by steam cars, and arrived in Salem, Massachusetts, early in August, where we hired a house, and occupied the same during the month. . . ." (*RLDS History of the Church*, Vol. 2, p. 464)

The Mormon prophet turned to his "seer stone" to validate the information provided by Burgess, as well as to feel out what "God" might think of their decision to embark upon such a journey. On 6 August 1836, Smith received the following reply from the "spirit world":

I, the Lord your God, am not displeased with your coming this journey, notwithstanding your follies. I have much treasure in this city for you . . . and its wealth pertaining to gold and silver shall be yours. Concern not yourselves about your debts, for I will give you power to pay them. . . . And inquire diligently concerning the more ancient inhabitants and founders of this city; For there are more treasures than one for you in this city. (*Latter Day Saints D&C*, Sec. 111.1-4)

It is highly significant to observe both the language and connotation of this "Salem Revelation." Joseph is instructed to inquire diligently of the more ancient inhabitants and founders of this city. "For there are more treasures than one for you in this city," Smith was counseled. These powers of darkness were eager for Joseph's return to Salem. (He had been sent there as a lad to recover from sickness.) Salem was and still is a special place of spiritist activity going back to its foundation in the sixteenth century. Perhaps what the "spirit" had in mind for Joseph was that he seek deep into the word that was given to him, for nesting in those promises were "spiritual treasures" which could not be found in the basement of a house. For over three hundred years Salem has been the witch capital of the United States.

It is obvious that Smith's yielding to the "false" revelation of the "hidden treasure" is due to his "god" not supplying his needs. There he is, found in the witch capital of the country, digging up the basement of a house in order to pay his debts. The gold (money) was not found, but perhaps the other treasures were. I have no doubt that Joseph sought them diligently as instructed through his "enchanted stone" while still in that city. Those who have studied the occult know that strict adherence to the spirits bring special favors. Not to adhere can bring severe consequences. Most Mormons do not like to discuss this "treasure hunt" revelation because it contains undeniable evidence that Joseph Smith was intoxicated with the treasure hunting spirit.

The "spirits" which had led him in Palmyra ten years before were still leading him, even into further forbidden paths of darkness that were awaiting him in the "city of the witches."

Soon after Joseph's return from Salem, clouds of darkness increased one-hundred-fold within the Mormon community. The spirits he apparently partook of there in Salem must have been those of confusion and destruction. For as atrocious as his leadership had been up till 1836, it became even worse during the next few years. Smith's leadership from 1836 to 1844 would bring death and devastation to thousands of his converts.

The only truth contained in the Salem revelation was that the "spirit" who gave it to Joseph was a "lying spirit." For the promise was, "I will give you power to pay them," [the debts] but Smith was unable to pay his debts as the spirit promised. His bank failed shortly after their return from Salem, and he and Rigdon had to flee to Missouri for fear of their lives. The Utah Mormon historian, Roberts, stated that the church in 1836 did indeed go to Salem seeking "earthly treasures" (*Comp. History of Church*, Vol., p. 412), that this was a prevalent mind-set among the Mormons is evidenced in a patriarchal blessing given to Wilford Woodruff in 1837, by Joseph Smith, Sr.: "Thou shalt have access to the treasures hid in the sand to assist thy necessities. An

angel of God shall show thee the treasures of the earth that
thou mayest have riches to assist thee in gathering many
orphan Children to Zion" (Woodruff, 1:143). This prophetic
promise was not fulfilled in the land of Zion (Jackson County,
Mo.), but perhaps it was in the salt sands of Utah.

These Mormon leaders who claim to be the "apple of
God's eye," the Lord's specially chosen endtime apostles, are
found "chasing" a fairy tale halfway across the United States
in 1836. Nowhere in the Bible is it recorded that a true
prophet of God ever yielded himself to such foolishness. But
what the Bible does promise is: "I have been young and now
am old; yet have I not seen the righteous forsaken, nor His
seed begging for bread" (Psalms 37:25).

The action of these Mormon leaders reflected a faith
totally foreign to the gospel that Jesus taught, where on one
occasion he told His disciples, ". . . take no thought, saying,
What shall we eat? or, What shall we drink? Wherewithal
shall we be clothed? (For after all these things do the Gentiles seek:) for your heavenly Father knoweth that ye have
need of all these things" (Matthew 6:31-32).

Perhaps there is no other moment in Mormon history
which reveals that Joseph Smith did not understand the
simple principal of faith in God than this trip to the city of
witches. It reveals how entrenched he was in casting his cares
upon the princes of this world.

CHAPTER FOURTEEN

The Greatest Fable Ever Told

❖

All of Mormonism shares one thing in perfect harmony with all its many factions, and that being the 1820 grove experience of Joseph Smith. It is this glorified "story" of the grove where the selling of the Mormon religion begins. This story pretends to tell how the Father and the Son left the throne of heaven and appeared to Smith to answer the question of which church he should join. He claimed to be confused as to whether he should join the Methodist, the Baptist, or the Presbyterian Church.

This 1820 story has for over 150 years been Mormonism's number one line of propaganda to sell their religion around the world. This 1820 story has been the master key in their brainwashing evangelism. This story presents Mormonism as the most divinely called and instituted religion the world has ever witnessed. They claim that from this one experience of Joseph Smith that they, of all people, hold the only true priesthood authority to represent God in all the world. They claim, from this one experience, that God bestowed upon their church the keys of salvation for this last dispensation, and that any who desires salvation must come unto their priesthood to be saved. Therefore, they present themselves as being the sole stewards of God's Kingdom in all this world. In this religion, a Christian is an infidel, and only Mormons are God's saints.

The finished product of this carefully designed 1820 grove story was finally completed by Joseph Smith in 1838. This was some eighteen years after its supposed occurrence. The first time any Mormons heard about such an event ever having taken place was in the year 1832. This was almost three years after the formation of the Mormon Church and twelve years after the event was to have happened. In 1832, when the story was first mentioned, Oliver Cowdery was engaged with Smith in writing a history of the rise of the Mormon Church. He states that the year was 1821 and not 1820. He further states that it was only the Lord who appeared to Smith, not the Father and Son, as Smith declared in 1838. Cowdery also states that Smith was sixteen-years-old and not fourteen as Smith reported in 1838.

In Joseph Smith's own diary of 1832, he describes only the Lord Jesus as having appeared to him in the year 1820, and reports his age as fifteen. In February of 1835 Oliver Cowdery is writing again in a publication called *The Messenger and Advocate*. Here Mormon history is being recorded under the supervision of Smith himself. This time they say it was a messenger from God that appeared to Smith. Now the year is 1822, and Smith is seventeen-years-old.

Joseph Smith in 1835 records in his own diary that the experience occurred in 1819, and that neither the Father or the Son was there, but instead there appeared many angels. He was fourteen-years-old this time. There were several other accounts written by key Mormons during this period, all of which conflict with the 1838 account, with none of them mentioning that the Father and the Son as having appeared to Joseph.

Why was there so much confusion over what was supposed to have been a very vivid, dramatic, and clear–cut visitation from two of the Supreme Rulers of the Universe? Why should it have taken Joseph Smith eighteen or nineteen years to finally arrive at what he concluded happened in the wooded grove near his home? Why would the Mormon leaders and historians believe that the story told in 1838 was more accurate than all the stories of 1832 or 1835? Any person should know that the older an event gets, the less remembered details; while the temptation to embellish is always lurking.

Previous to 1838 Smith could not decide whether it should be angels or the Son of God at his grove experience. The mass confusion by Smith, etal., in attempting to compose the 1820 grove experience shows that a fable was certainly in the making. He definitely was not at this point giving any thought that the day would come when someone would be able to view all the various versions at one time. It also shows that Smith was careless and failed to carefully protect the deception he was further fostering. To change the body of an experience from "Many Angels," or a "Messenger," to that of the Father and the Son represents in Smith's thinking of an escalation of his own calling—a calling which would serve to enhance his own spiritual authority among the Mormons. The thought of having a leader who was visited by the Father and Son would awesomely affect the minds of his followers and would further distance him from any rivals in the rising Mormon empire.

Smith became an artist in creating glorified images of himself and his supposed calling. In the New Testament account of Jesus, there exists the deepest of divine significance concerning the details which surrounded His birth, ministry, and resurrection, but not one time was there recorded that the Father left Heaven to visit His only Begotten Son and speak with Him in Person. But as Smith and the Mormons would have the world to believe, it is that Smith's calling was so special that God would do for Smith something He had never done before. That was to personally visit a mortal man face to face. In order for God to do such a thing He would have to deny His own Word.

The Bible is very clear on this point. God told Moses, "Thou canst not see My Face: for there shall *no man see me and live*" (*emphasis* mine, Exodus 33:20). Yet Smith tells the world that *he* did at the age of fourteen(?) and got away with it, if you believe the story Mormons tell.

In 1832 Smith himself stated in one of his revelations

that no man could see the face of God and live without the covering of the Mormon Melchizedek priesthood. (*UT D&C*, Sec. 84, verses 21-22). Well Smith certainly had a relapse of memory in 1838, when he wrote of himself looking upon the face of God in the year 1820, because he did not enact this special supernatural buffer until after 1830. Therefore, had he looked upon the face of God in 1820 as he claims, Smith would have perished and Mormonism would have never been born.

During the years of 1815-1830 there were several experiences reported in the local newspapers very similar to the one Smith reported as having. It seemed, back then, that reporting such spiritual experiences made for good news. Now, according to Smith, he had spread his story around to a good number of people, including the ministers. But somehow Smith's glorious experience, which far outshone them all, failed to ever make the papers. But what a story that would have made, "Fourteen-year-old visited by the Father and Son." Such an experience would have been the most sensational of all news and would have spread throughout the entire area of western New York.

Smith wrote in 1838 that his experience caused a great uproar:

> I soon found however that my telling the story had excited a great deal of prejudice against me among professors of religion and was the cause of great persecution which continued to increase, and though I was an obscure boy only between fourteen and fifteen years of age and my circumstances in life such as to make a boy of no consequence in the world; yet men of high standing would take notice sufficient to excite the public mind against me and create a hot persecution, and this was common among all the sects: all united to persecute me. (*History of Joseph Smith*, *Times and Seasons*, Vol. 3, No. 11, pp. 748-749)

There is no way that this wide-spread persecution against Smith could have passed totally unnoticed by everyone in Smith's community. Such an uproar in the small town of Palmyra would have made the headlines of its paper, *The Wayne Sentinel*. There was not one word ever spoken nor recorded except by Smith, who would finally report it all in 1838. This wondrous thing would even bypass the ears of his own mother, Lucy Smith. When she wrote the history of their family, she did not give the slightest intimation of any such event having taken place in 1820. What she did was to take Smith's 1842 account in the *Times and Seasons* and drop it into her book as part of their family history. But casual reading will reveal that it is out of place.

It is absolutely certain that she had no knowledge that God the Father and His Son ever told her son Joseph that every church on earth was an abomination and that he was to join none of them. A study of her writing reveals that such a dramatic event in her family never occurred, and that she had no knowledge that her son was soon to be God's instrument in restoring His Kingdom on earth.

If Lucy had been aware of Joseph's calling to shortly set up the Lord's Church, she would not have joined the Presbyterian Church in 1825. She and some of her children would remain members of this church until September 1828, almost one year after Smith was to have begun work on the Book of Mormon, which would bring the "True Church" into being.

In the month of June 1828, Joseph Smith attempted to join the Methodist Episcopal Church in Harmony, Pennsylvania. Smith is found defying the direct command of God, "join none of them for they are all an abomination in My sight." During this time a portion of the Book of Mormon had been completed and Smith was on his way to setting up "The Mormon Kingdom Upon The Earth." Yet Smith was attempting to seek after light and truth from one of those "abominable" (in his revelation) churches.

Smith's efforts to join the Methodist church in Harmony was reported by Joseph Lewis, one of Emma's first cousins. The report is as follows:

> The facts are these: I with Joshua McKune, a local preacher at that time, I think in June, 1828, heard on Saturday, that Joe Smith had joined the church on Wednesday afternoon. . . . We thought it was a disgrace to the church to have a practicing necromancer, a dealer

in enchantments and bleeding ghosts, in it. So on Sunday we . . . talked with him some time . . . before the meeting. Told him that his occupation, habits, and moral character were at variance with the discipline, that his name would be a disgrace to the church, that there should have been recantation, confession, and at least promised reformation—That he could that day publicly ask that his name be stricken from the class book, or stand an investigation. He chose the former, and did that very day make the request that his name be taken off the class-book . . ." (*Amboy Journal*, 11 June 1879).

Joseph Smith's desire to join the Methodist church in Harmony, Pennsylvania, indicted himself. He in this one act sealed the fact of history, that God never told him to join none of them, for they were all wrong, and that all their creeds were an abomination in his sight; that their professors were all corrupt." The above account given by his wife's close cousin demonstrates the clearest of evidence that the 1820 grove experience not only did not occur, but that Joseph Smith was a deceiver of the worse kind. The church which he established was rather a church which was an abomination in the sight of God.

The 1820 grove experience has become the chief cornerstone upon which Mormonism's claims of divine authority is founded. The Book of Mormon was a great lie indeed. But the greatest lie of all that Mormonism ever perpetrated is the fabricated fable that God the Father left His throne in Heaven to visit a young man which had just entered the apprentice stages of the occult. Many precious souls over the years have come to believe this lie with convictions far deeper than they would ever hold for the Bible itself.

CHAPTER FIFTEEN

Joseph Smith's Bout with His Father-in-Law

❖

During 1827, the Mormons tell us that Joseph was spiritually preparing himself for the purpose of receiving the Book of Mormon plates. Yet Smith thought nothing of "hijacking" his bride-to-be after he had been denied—in very plain language—her hand in marriage by her father. The word that was out in Harmony, Pennsylvania, was that Smith had "bewitched" the daughter of Isaac Hale. A close neighbor of the Hales had this to say in the *History of Susquehanna County, Pennsylvania* (Emily C. Blackman, Philadelphia, p. 103): "Their daughter Emma was intelligent, and, that she should marry Joseph Smith, Jr., the Mormon leader, can only be accounted for by supposing 'he had bewitched her,' as he afterward bewitched the masses."

According to one of Smith's neighbors, Smith had been ordered by the demon spirit Moroni to bring Emma Hale to Cumorah on the night he was to receive the treasure. This was a strict condition that this spirit had placed upon Smith. This spirit had been requiring that Smith bring someone with him each year since 1824. There is one possible way Moroni, or the spirit which Joseph communed with through his "seer stone," could have developed interest in Emma, and that would have been through the conversations of Smith and Luman Walters. Walters was for a long time

seeking to obtain the same treasure along with Samuel
Lawrence. Emma was a cousin of Walters, and Smith had
been a boarder at her father's home. Between the two, the
"spirit" ascertained enough information about Emma that
he desired to put Smith through another trying ordeal before bursting Smith's treasure bubble.

Joseph Knight, a friend of the Smiths, told of Smith's
plight of trying to appease Moroni.

> The spirit told him that if he would do right according
> to the will of God, he might obtain [the treasure] the
> 22nd day of September next [1827] and if not he never
> would have them . . . Then he [Smith] looked in his glass
> and found it was Emma Hale, daughter of old Mr. Hail
> of Pensylvany, a girl that he had seen before, for he had
> bin down there before with me. (Jessee 1976, p. 31-32;
> Hartley, p. 21)

Smith, in his desperation, apparently could come to only
one conclusion and that was to somehow marry her, if he
could. He knew of no other way in which he could get her
to the "hill." Smith would lay his plans through an old money-
digging friend of his named Josiah Stowell. From there on all
the circumstances surrounding his marriage with Emma Hale
would be suspicious indeed. He would break with a long-
time family tradition and marry too young. Joseph arranges
with his friend Josiah Stowell to have Emma come and visit
him and then he would show up after she had arrived. Smith
would have to slip into town without the law knowing he was
there, since he was told not to be found in that area after his
1826 trial. Smith would obtain Stowell's help to break down
Emma's resistance of guilt in defying her family's wishes.
Smith blatantly disrespected Emma's father, who had threat-
ened his life if he did not leave his daughter Emma alone.

To what extent Smith may have used his talismatic power
upon Emma, only a discreetly few would have known. As
desperate as he was to obtain a cache of treasure after so
many long years of seeking, I am convinced he would have
used everything in his arsenal to have gotten her to that
"hill." Bewitching Emma was probably Smith's number one
strategy which he had in mind before leaving Palmyra.

Lorenzo Saunders wrote of Emma, "Joseph's wife was a

pretty woman, just as pretty a woman as I ever saw. When she came to the Smiths she was disappointed and used to come down to our house and sit down and cry. Said she was deceived and had got into a hard place" (Fawn Brodie, *No Man Knows My History*, p. 42).

The *History of Susquehanna* recorded a little on Emma's father on page 103:

> It is thought that Mr. Hale was a little deluded at first, as well as others, in regards to Joe's prophecy of the existence of precious minerals, when digging was progressing in the vicinity, under the latter's direction, and the party were boarding at Mr. Hale's, but his common sense soon manifested itself, and his disapproval of Joe was notorious. He was a man of forethought and generosity.

The account of Joseph and Emma's first return home to her fathers several months after their marriage was described by a friend of Joseph's, Peter Ingersoll, who was driving the wagon that carried them back to Harmony, Pennsylvania, from Palmyra, New York.

> When we arrived at Mr. Hale's in Harmony, PA., from which place he had taken his wife, a scene presented itself truly affecting. His father-in-law [Mr. Hale] addressed Joseph, in a flood of tears: "You have stolen my daughter, and married her. I had much rather have followed her to her grave. You spend your time in digging for money—pretend to see in a stone and thus try to deceive people." Joseph wept, and acknowledged he could not see in a stone now, nor never could; and that his former pretensions in that respect, were all false. He then promised to give up his old habits of digging for money and looking into stones. Mr. Hale told Joseph, if he would move to Pennsylvania and work for a living, he would assist him in getting into business. Joseph acceded to this proposition. (Charles A. Shook, *The True Origin Of The Book Of Mormon*, Cincinnati, Ohio, The Standard Publishing Co., p. 20)

We see this great emotional outbreak of Joseph was all a front. Many times tears reflect deep sincerity and reform, but not in Smith's case. He seemed to always prevaricate that which was expedient for the moment. Joseph is quoted as saying he would give up stone gazing to his father-in-law, Mr. Hale, which he did not do! He states that he could not see in a "stone" nor ever could. Well he sure was a long time looking into a "stone" where nothing could be seen! He used one from 1819 till 1832; later he uses it in Nauvoo to translate the Egyptian Papyri, which was later printed in another Mormon bible called "The Pearl Of Great Price." A man who would lie and deceive his wife and her own father would lie to anybody.

Joseph's father-in-law, Isaac Hale, first met Joseph in November 1825. According to Mr. Hale's own words,

> . . . He was at that time in the employ of a set of men who were called "money-diggers," and his occupation was that of seeing, or pretending to see by means of a stone placed in his hat, and his hat closed over his face. In this way he pretended to discover minerals and hidden treasure. His appearance at this time, was that of a careless young man—not very well educated, and very saucy and insolent to his father. Smith, and his father, with several other "money-diggers," boarded at my house while they were employed in digging for a mine that they supposed had been opened and worked by the Spaniards, many years since. Young Smith gave the "money-diggers" great encouragement, at first, but when they had arrived in digging, to near the place they then became discouraged, and soon after dispersed. Here he had stated an immense treasure would be found—he said the enchantment was so powerful that he could not see.
> . . . (Ibid., p. 31)

In 1827, some time after Joseph talked Emma into meeting him at Josiah Stowell's over in New York, Isaac Hale continues his account on page 32 (Ibid.): "Smith stated to me, that he had given up what he called 'glass-looking,' and that he expected to work hard for a living, and was willing to do so." But to Mr. Hale's dismay, he soon learns that Joseph was back to his old "hat tricks." Isaac writes, ". . . The manner in which he pretended to read and interpret, was the same as when he looked for the money-diggers, with the stone in his hat, and his hat over his face, while the Book of Plates was at the same time hid in the woods!" (Ibid, p. 33).

Hale concludes with the following observation on the same page, ". . . the whole Book of Mormon (so callêd) is a silly fabrication of falsehood and wickedness, got up for speculation, and with a design to dupe the credulous and unwary—and in order that its fabricators may live upon the spoils of those who swallow the deception." Isaac Hale affirmed this before Charles Dimon, justice of peace, 20 March 1834.

Joseph Smith's arrest and trial of 1826 has already been spoken of in an earlier chapter. In the fall of 1825 Josiah Stowell traveled from Bainbridge, Chenango County, New York, in an effort to hire Joseph Jr. for the purpose of helping him search for hidden treasures he and others believed to be buried.

> The place where the treasure was supposed to lie buried was on the place now owned by J. M. Tillman, near the McKune farm, then the property of Wm. Hale. (Dale Morgan, *Dale Morgan On Early Mormons*, p. 325)

> The following agreement, the original of which is in the possession of a citizen of Thompson township, was discovered by our correspondent, and forwarded to us as a matter of local interest:

> The existence of the "buried treasures" referred to was "revealed" to Joe Smith Jr., who with his father the Prophet, at that time resided on what is now known as the McCune farm, about two miles down the river from this place, and upon the strength of which revelation a stock company was organized to dig for the aforesaid treasure. After the company was organized, a second communication was received by Joseph, Jr., from the "other world", advising the treasure seekers to suspend operations, as it was necessary for one of the company to die before the treasure could be secured.

> Harper the peddler, who was murdered soon after, near the place where the Catholic cemetery in this borough is now located, was one of the original members of the company, and his death was regarded by the remainder of the band as a Providential occurrence, which the

"powers" had brought about for their special benefit.
The death of Harper having removed the only obstacle
in the way of success, the surviving members recom-
menced operations, and signed an "agreement," giving
the widow Harper the half (sic) of one-third of all the
treasures secured. The following is the agreement, written by the old humbug, Joseph Smith, (Sr.) himself. . . .
(Ibid, p. 324)

The articles of agreement appear on page 325 in Dale
Morgan's book, *Dale Morgan on Early Mormons*. The agreement was made in the Township of Harmony, Pennsylvania,
1 November 1825. The parties to the agreement are listed
on the same page and were as follows: Isaac Hale, Charles
A. Newton, David Hale, Joseph Smith, Sr., Senator P. Newton, Josiah Stowell, Calvin Stowell, Joseph Smith, Jr., and
William I. Wiley. There were three others which were to
receive of the bounty, but were not signers of the agreement.

The foregoing is conclusive evidence that the Mormon
prophet, Joseph Smith, Jr., was involved in a very shady
treasure search, while according to all Mormon histories, he
was spiritually preparing himself to receive the "Holy Plates"
from Hill Cumorah.

During the six months of this ordeal Joseph was board-
ing at the home of Isaac Hale along with his father and
perhaps others. Although Mr. Hale initially signed the agreement, he was to shortly thereafter pull out. Isaac Hale had
ample opportunity to come to know his future son-in-law
very well during this six month episode. He definitely saw
several things about this young "romancer of the stone"
which caused him to strongly reject Joseph when he later
asked for his daughter's hand in marriage.

The search for this treasure dragged on for several
months, and apparently the only person to financially benefit from the dig was Joseph Smith, Jr. The only labor he was
performing was looking at the "stone" and passing on the
digging orders, as well as reporting on the movement of the
spirits in charge of the treasures.

The sons of Josiah Stowell soon became suspicious of
young Joseph and his methods and brought charges against

Smith. These charges gave rise to the Bainbridge trial of 1826, the trial Mormons had denied existing since 1830.

Joseph, being under a very strong spell of his "spirit guides," could neither please his wife, nor his father-in-law. There were times that he seemed to really wish to do so and go straight but was too deep into the underworld of deception to just walk free. His "crystal gazing" was no longer fun and games; he had become a marked man for the devil's plan.

The stage was now set in Joseph's mind to not only lie to the world, but to God. The "deceiving spirits" had so conditioned his heart that he was willing to produce a book and call it the very "Word of God." He was willing to say that God Himself had left Heaven and met with him in Palmyra, New York, and that God had sent special angels to present the materials to him. He would go so far as to say that it would be translated by the very "Power of God Himself." He was so under the influence of these suggestive powers that he could think no less of himself than as being the greatest prophet ever to walk this earth.

It is this man Joseph Smith that the Mormons hold before the world as a shining example of one of God's greatest prophets. They have exalted his word above the Bible, as well as the Son of God. They will tell you that if you have any chance for salvation you must bow down to Smith's priesthood and receive of his doctrines. There was one man who knew Smith for what he was; a liar, a deceiver, and a false prophet. That man was his father-in-law, Isaac Hale.

CHAPTER SIXTEEN

The Riddle of the "Lost" 116 Pages

❖

This chapter may interest Mormons more than any other chapter of the book. It will require a great deal of concentration—if your concentration breaks down there is a summary at the end of the chapter to help bring it back into perspective.

Here we will delve into the "unknown mystery" of the "lost" 116 pages of the Book of Mormon. This chapter will show that Smith did not lose the source material from which he created the first 116 pages, but that he would place portions of this original material elsewhere in the Book of Mormon. The blunders he made in the rewriting of these "lost" pages places an irrefutable mark of human origin upon the Book of Mormon.

Martin Harris was scribing for Joseph Smith in the spring of 1828 when he asked Joseph to allow him to take the 116 pages of the Book of Mormon, which they had just completed writing, back home with him to Palmyra. While in Palmyra, Martin seemed to be finding great satisfaction in showing and reading these pages to any who desired to see or hear them. But one day the pages strangely came up missing from his home while in Palmyra. The story has it that his wife "torched" them. Therefore this portion of the Book of Mormon has become known as the "lost" 116 pages.

Since 1830 their disappearance has caused much speculation among the Mormons as to what may have been written upon them. The mystery of these 116 pages has a great deal of light shed upon them by Joseph's excessive infatuation with the "secret societies." Further light is shed in blunders he made regarding his special divining instruments called "interpreters," as well as a vast number of parallels which exist between two suspect portions within the Book of Mormon.

During the late 1820s there was a wave of anti-Masonry which swept through western New York, including Smith's hometown. The cause was over the murder of an ex-Mason named Morgan.* The Masons were referred to in his local papers as "secret combinations." I am of the opinion that the "lost" 116 pages had within its text extensive exegesis on Masonry with warning of their works of darkness and their destructive "secret combinations." Since Joseph claimed in the Book of Mormon that both the Nephites and Jaredites were destroyed by these "secret combinations," it is very probable that Joseph was showing in the "lost" 116 pages how Jerusalem would be destroyed by them, and he was warning the Nephites and present America of the coming destruction at the hands of these "secret societies." I believe Joseph chose to insert this anti-Masonic material with the purpose in mind of not only showing how prophetic his book was, but also to create a favorable acceptance of it.

Interpreters

The purpose of "interpreters" (seer stones), according to the Book of Mormon, was for discovering the "secret works of darkness" and for interpreting unknown languages. The problem with Smith's "interpreters" was that he wound up with *two separate sets* of them in the Book of Mormon, with no explanation of how the God of Heaven provided for one of the sets. Only God could make "interpreters," you see!

In the original manuscript before it was lost, Smith had

---

*Mrs. Morgan would later become one of Joseph Smith's polygamous wives in Nauvoo, Illinois. Smith was a powerful Mason at the time of this marriage.

to have Lehi, the first prophet, possess a set of the "interpreters," in order for the following Book of Mormon history
to be accurate: "King Mosiah (a descendant of Lehi) . . . took
the plates of Brass . . . all the records and also the Interpreters, and conferred them upon him, (Alma)" and that he
should also hand "them down from one generation to another, even as they had been handed down from the time
that Lehi left Jerusalem" (B.M., Mosiah 28:20).

So we see from the book of Mosiah that the interpreters
were supposed to be in Lehi's possession around the time he
left Jerusalem. But in I Nephi no mention is made of the
interpreters in the section which replaced the "lost" 116
pages. The interpreters were not among the records (etc.)
that Nephi took from the Treasury of Jerusalem in 600 B.C.
They certainly would have recorded a special visitation from
God if He had given them a set. One of the main uses of
these special stones, besides interpreting unknown languages,
was "discovering" the "secret works of darkness," the "secret
combinations" among the people. It is very probable in the
original manuscript of the "lost" 116 pages that Smith had
Lehi utilizing the interpreters to discover the "secret works
of darkness" going on in his hometown of Jerusalem. He
then took the knowledge he received through this means to
warn the inhabitants of their destruction.

This strange mystery created by Joseph Smith can only
be accounted for in the episode of the "lost" 116 pages in
that he relocated portions of it near the end of his book and
titled it the book of Ether. For we find in the Book of Ether
both the interpreters and the "secret combinations." Since
Joseph only used a portion of the "lost" 116 pages to compose the book of Ether, it is probably the reason why we
read in the first verse of this book these words, "Behold, I
give not the full account, but a part of the account I give"
(Book of Mormon, Ether 1:5). So Joseph only gave a part of
the account which he had written on the 116 pages that was
lost.

In western New York in the 1820s you were called a
"seer" if you were a "glass looker," or one who possessed
certain "stones" through which you could receive revelations
or see treasures beneath the earth. In the outset of the Book

of Mormon the "Mormon Seer" exalts this occult ritual of his into a high and lofty divine procedure and portrays it as being instituted by God. In the book of Ether we read of God talking to his prophet, "And behold, these two stones will I give thee, and ye shall seal them up also, with the things ye shall write . . . In my own due time these stones shall magnify to the eyes of men, these things which ye shall write" (B.M., Ether 3:23-24). This all occurred around 2200 B.C. in the Book of Mormon.

(The Book of Ether contains a brief history of a group of people called the Jaredites, who migrated to America from the Tower of Babel in 2200 B.C.)

Some 2,000 years later in the time of a King Mosiah around 200 B.C. we learn that a certain group of Nephites had found a large stone. The account reads, ". . . in the days of Mosiah, there was a large stone brought unto him, with engravings on it; and he did interpret the gravings, by the gift and power of God" (B.M., Omni 1:20). What did this Mosiah use in order to interpret the stone? The answer is found seventy-five or eighty years later when we read of his grandson, King Mosiah, where another finding has been made; this time it is a set of twenty-four gold plates. The people who had found them were inquiring from a stranger named Ammon (sent by King Mosiah) who had come into their midst if he knew anyone who could interpret the plates. His reply was, ". . . I can assuredly tell thee, O King, of a man that can translate the records; for he has wherewith that he can look, and translate all records that are of ancient date; and it is a gift from God. And the things are called interpreters, and no man can look in them except he be commanded, lest he should look for that he be ought not, and he should perish. And who–so–ever is commanded to look in them, the same is called seer" (B.M., Mosiah 5:73-74).

For King Mosiah to possess a set of interpreters, he would have to have inherited them through the kings, back to the time of Lehi. But Joseph loses track and leaves the interpreters in the material he uses to create the Book of Ether. So the Brother of Jared runs off with Lehi's instrument of divination and takes it back in time some 1,600 years.

A. Smith got the kings confused in the Book of Ether, when he had his last historian of the Book of Mormon write that it was King Benjamin who received the twenty-four plates and interpreters, when it should have been his son, King Mosiah. This mistake resulted when Smith was attempting to reconstruct the "lost" 116 pages into the Book of Ether and then tie the Ancient Jaredites of Ether back into the Nephite History.

B. Smith stated in the Book of Ether that King Benjamin (Mosiah?) was to keep the twenty-four gold plates and interpreters and was not to allow them to come into the world. It reads: "For this cause did King Benjamin keep them that they should not come unto the world until after Christ should show himself unto his people. And after Christ . . . shewed himself . . . he commanded that they [twenty-four plates and interpreters] should not be made manifest" (B.M., Ether 1:95-96). According to Smith then, in the Book of Ether, the interpreters and the twenty-four plates were "forbidden" to be shown to anybody.

C. But Smith errs and has King Mosiah, not Benjamin, get these "forbidden" twenty-four gold plates and translates them. "Forbidden"—"ought not to be translated"—yet, the seer did not "perish" for translating things he ought not (B.M., Jacob 2:44-47). The reason given as to why King Mosiah translated the twenty-four gold plates was because of the great anxiety of his people, for they were desirous beyond measure to know concerning those people (Jaredites) who had been destroyed (B.M., Mosiah 12:16-18). When Mosiah made the translation, he translated the whole record, he made no mention of translating just a part of it, and Smith wrote no stipulations about it either. King Mosiah had full liberty. Smith failed to have God warn King Mosiah of the "forbidden" condition! (B.M., Mosiah 12:22).

D. This was a great blunder indeed by Joseph Smith to allow King Mosiah to translate the "forbidden" revelations of the brother of Jared from the twenty-four gold plates of the history of the Jaredites, and read it unto the people 125 years before God's command said that it could be done.

E. The second blunder was that the twenty-four gold plates contained the "mysteries" and the "works of darkness," and their "secret words," or the "secret works" of those people, who had been destroyed (the Jaredites); a similar warning existed, ". . . that you retain them from the people, and they know them not" (B.M., Alma 117:52-59). Yet Smith allows this occult perverted information to be translated and read to the Nephite people by King Mosiah.

Again these two unimaginable blunders were: one, he allows the seer, King Mosiah, to read the "sealed" revelation, which was not to be read until 125 years later when the Lord was to appear. The second was to allow the "forbidden knowledge" of the "secret works of darkness" to be read unto the people.

The reason Smith had this occult knowledge given back to the Nephites was so that his original plot could be carried out. The original plot was that these "secret societies" of the Nephites would eventually bring about the destruction of the Nephite people. But when the "secret combinations" appeared in the Nephite society there is not one word that indicates the "secret society" was formed from the knowledge that was on the twenty-four plates.

The only answer that appeals to reason as to why King Mosiah, the "Nephite Seer," did not understand these vital details is that Mosiah was a robot character of Smith and company, and Mosiah could only play out what Smith scripted him to do. When Smith relocated, as well as reworked, the "secret combination" section ("lost" 116 pages) in forming the Book of Ether he could not keep track of all the specific details, even though he was supposed to be translating all of it by the "Power" of God.

According to Smith's last historian, Moroni, there were only twenty-four Jaredite plates. Moroni writes, "and I take mine account from the twenty and four plates which were found by the people of Limhi, which is called the Book of Ether" (B.M., Ether 1:2).

A Possible Sequence

1. Joseph Smith had the first 116 pages of his new work stolen.

2. Knowing at some point and time in his book that he would introduce another set of people more ancient than

the Nephites, he revised the 116 pages and called it the Book of Ether (a short history of the Jaredite people.).

3. He chose to enter these people into the later Nephite history through the finding of a big stone and twenty-four gold plates, which contained historical data of the Jaredites.

4. Proof that Joseph had not created the name of this people at the time of Mosiah was that when the translation of the twenty-four "sealed" plates were made by Mosiah there was no mention of who the people were. To the Nephites, who were Hebrews, if you did not possess a name you were a "nobody." What was determined in the mind of Joseph at this time was that he would introduce a people that would come from the "Tower of Babel," but at this point in time he had not decided upon a name for them.

5. The Nephites in the "lost" 116 pages had interpreters. This is evident in that Mosiah had a set of interpreters, which were to be handed down from generation to generation (B.M., Mosiah 1 12:19). Therefore, it is easy to prove then that Lehi did possess them in the "lost" 116 pages (See B.M., Mosiah 13:2.).

6. But when Joseph removed the "lost" 116 pages of material* to the rear of the Book of Mormon, what is seen is that the brother of Jared, who originally was Lehi in the "lost" 116 pages, became the possessor of Lehi's interpreters. Joseph failed to reconcile this problem by giving Lehi some more interpreters when he replaced the "lost" pages. (That is, when he re-wrote the first few chapters of the Book of Mormon.)

7. Since the Book of Ether would be written several weeks after the Book of Mosiah, Joseph could not provide the name (Jaredites) as yet. He also had not determined what he was going to do about the "secret combinations," as well as the revelation of the brother of Jared. Therefore Mosiah was shown to break a verbal command from the mouth of Jesus and translate the twenty-four plates.

8. By the time Joseph had written in (RLDS) Alma 17:52 approximately twenty years after King Mosiah had translated

---

* Smith still had in his possession the manuscript from which the lost portion has been composed.

the "24 gold plates," he decided to mention the "secret combinations." But there was no mention of the "secret society" when Mosiah translated the plates. Now Alma was not a seer, although he had in his possession two sets of interpreters (the brother of Jared and Mosiah). He had nothing to interpret, so he was not a seer. But in Alma 37:21, which reads as an interesting insertion, "And now, I will speak unto you concerning those twenty-four plates, that ye keep them, that the 'mysteries' and the 'works of darkness,' and their 'secret works,' or the 'secret works' of those people, who have been destroyed, may be made manifest unto this people . . ." Surely there is an error in this paragraph because in verse 59 Alma exhorts his son to "retain (this information) from this people, that they know them not . . ." (B.M., Alma 17:29).

Joseph definitely made a grave blunder when he chose to have the knowledge of "secret combinations" pass from the ancient Jaredites to the Nephites through the instrument of God's prophet. A true prophet of God would instantly be repulsed by the thought of transmitting occult knowledge. This act is not only totally out of nature but was a very poorly designed scheme. But for Smith it was probably justified in his mind; as he later would become a chief in this "secret society" which he seems to condemn in the Book of Mormon. (He became a 33d Degree Plus Mason in Nauvoo in one day.)

That the "lost" 116 pages or portions of it were obviously transferred over to the Book of Ether is further confirmed in the similarities between it and the reconstructed first chapter of I Nephi, as it now appears in the Book of Mormon. It is not surprising that the similarities exist since Joseph was attempting to reconstruct the same story over again. Some of the more noticeable similarities are as follows:

1. Both Lehi and brother of Jared crying unto the Lord—Both leaders remind you of the Moses account in the Bible.

2. Both received a revelation of Jesus.

3. Both Nephi and brother of Jared are large in stature.

4. Both brought out their families and some other families with them.

5. Both go up into a mountain.

6. Both receive special divining instruments—Lehi, a ball with spindles.

7. Both build boats/ships instructed by God.

8. Both had honey to take with them.

9. Both were led into a wilderness.

10. Both were going to a "choice land."

11. Both were given extensive revelations which included the very end-times.

12. Both did "molten" ore.

13. Both stories are characteristic of the Israelites in the wilderness.

14. Both went to a "land of promise" or "promised land."

15. Both had tents to pitch.

16. Both gave names to the places they dwelt.

17. Both Nephi and brother Jared were shown great things by God in the mountains.

18. Both boats/ships were driven by the wind.

19. Both were driven toward a "promised land," then both were made to land upon the shore of the "promised land."

20. Both began to "till the earth" (Ether 6:13, I Nephi 18:24).

21. Both praised the Lord "all the day long."

There is only one conclusion left to be drawn, and that is Smith relocated a portion of these "lost" 116 pages to the rear of the Book of Mormon, and named it the Book of Ether. Again he selected a name with an occult "ling," *Ether*, coming from ethereal—airy, shadowy, subtle, vaporous, and ghostly.

In summary: When King Mosiah transfers the guardianship of the Nephite records, interpreters (and etc.), to Alma II, the king informs him that these things had been handed down from generation to generation dating back to the time that Lehi left Jerusalem in 600 B.C. (B.M., Mosiah 13:1,2). It was twenty years later when this Alma would tell his son Helaman that the interpreters, now called "a stone" or "directors," would shine forth into darkness and discover these "secret combinations."

1. The above says Mosiah had gotten his information from his father, etc., all the way back to Lehi in Jerusalem.

2. Alma had gotten his information about discovering these "dark combinations" from King Mosiah.

3. Lehi, then, must have been the one who had used the interpreters to discover the secret combinations in Jerusalem, or else where could Alma have gotten his knowledge?

4. Because there isn't anywhere else in the Book of Mormon where the interpreters were used for that purpose up to that time. The only place it could have happened was with Lehi at Jerusalem. This information is nowhere else to be found or accounted for, except that Smith in the lost 116 pages had Lehi use the interpreter stones to discover the secret combinations in Jerusalem. But there is not the slightest suggestion in the Book of Mormon that there were any secret combinations in Jerusalem. What happened to them?

Joseph, being unwilling to reproduce the same lost 116 pages over again in fear of discrepancies, moved the secret combinations to the Jaredites, by which they would be destroyed.

The proof that the Book of Ether is composed of the lost 116 pages is when Alma tells his son, Helaman, that the purpose of the stones is to discover the secret combinations. Since there were no secret combinations from Alma's time back to Lehi's time, the only place one can turn to find the origin of the stones and secret combinations is in the Book of Ether. They should have been traceable to Lehi but cannot be traced back to him in the present state of the Book of Mormon. In the original lost 116 pages, they could have been traced back to Lehi, for the interpreters or stones would have been in Lehi's possession and he would be seen as using them to "discover the secret works of darkness about to destroy Jerusalem."

The Path of the Two Sets of Interpreters

The lost 116 Pages definitely contained a set of interpreters. This is borne out because a set of interpreters appears later in the Nephite history.

But in the replacement of the lost 116 pages (1 Nephi) Smith fails to make any mention of this most "spiritual instrument of divination."

Smith's great blunder came when he had the one set of interpreters go in two different directions, with two separate civilizations.

The one set of interpreters travels from the original lost 116 pages

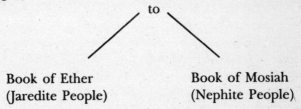

Book of Ether   Book of Mosiah
(Jaredite People)   (Nephite People)

Then, Smith has the Jaredite Set hidden and later found, and this set eventually winds up in the hands of King Mosiah. Now, the King has two sets. The scenario of the interpreters, along with the twenty-four gold plates, confirms that Joseph Smith was devoid of the intelligence of God; he was not authoring his own book but was obviously endeavoring to reconstruct the writings of someone else.

CHAPTER SEVENTEEN

1844 View of Nauvoo— Joseph's City

❖

The following letter was written by Isaac and Sarah Hall Scott just a few weeks before Joseph Smith met his death at Carthage, Illinois. This young lady was a recent convert to Mormonism and had moved from Massachusetts in 1843 to Nauvoo, Illinois. She had written a series of letters to her in-laws during this period of time. These letters will uncover much of the truth which all Mormon leaders have covered up and in most part have kept from the world, as well as from their own people. This letter confirms what many either suspicioned or knew concerning the Mormon leaders during the days of Nauvoo.

Vicinity of Nauvoo.
June 16, 1844.

My dear Father and Mother:

For such I suppose I may call you, on account of the relationship that now exist between us. Altho far distant, and having never had the privilege of beholding your faces, yet I rejoice exceedingly in the pleasure which I this day enjoy of sitting down to write a few lines to two so near and dear to me as you are. I have greatly desired to see you since I became acquainted with your daughter, and adopted into your family. But I have had to do with only hearing from you thus far. By a letter that Mrs. Haven received from you a few days since, we have the pleasing intelligence that you are all well, which blessing we also enjoy. I am glad that I ever became united to your family, for by this step I have gotten what Solomon says is a good thing. He says he that hath gotten a wife from the Lord, hath gotten a good thing. So say I. And were not for troubles that exist in the land, we would rejoice continually.

But because of the things that are and have been taught in the Church of Latter Day Saints for two years past which now assume a portentous aspect, I say because of these things we are in trouble. And were it not that we wish to give you a fair unbiased statement of facts as they really exist, we perhaps would not have written you so soon. But we feel it to be our duty to let you know how things are going on in this land of boasted liberty, this Sanctum-Sanctorum of all the earth, the city of Nauvoo. The Elders will likely tell you a different tale from what I shall as they are positively instructed to deny these things abroad. But it matters not to us what they say: our object is to state to you the truth, for we do not want to be guilty of deceiving any one. We will now give you a correct statement of the doctrines that are taught and practised in the Church according to our own knowledge. We will mention three in particular.

A plurality of Gods. A plurality of living wives. And unconditional sealing up to external life against all sins save the shedding of innocent blood or consenting there unto. These with many other things are taught by Joseph, which we consider are odious and doctrines of devils.

Joseph says there are Gods above the god of this universe as far as he is above us, and if he should transgress the laws given to Him by those above Him, He would be hurled from his Throne to hell, as was Lucifer and all his creations with him. But God says there is no other God but himself. Moses says he is the Almighty God, and there is none other. David says he knows of no other God. The Apostles and Prophets almost all testify the same thing.

Joseph had a revelation last summer purporting to be

from the Lord, allowing the saints the privilege of having ten living wives at one time, I mean certain conspicuous characters among them. They do not content themselves with young women, but have seduced married women. I believe hundreds have been deceived. Now should I yield up your daughter to such wretches?

Mr. Haven knows these statements are correct, for they have been taught in the quorum to which he belongs by the highest authority in the Church. He has told me that he does not believe in these teachings but he does not come out and oppose them; he thinks that it will all come out right. But we think God never has nor never will sanction such proceedings, for we believe he has not changed; he says, "I am God I change not." These thing we can not believe, and it is by Sarah's repeated request that I write this letter.

Those who can not swallow down these things and came out and opposed the doctrine publicly, have been cut off from the Church without any lawful process whatever. They were not notified to trial neither were they allowed the privilege of being present to defend themselves; neither was any one permitted to speak on their behalf. They did not know who was their judge or jury until it was all over and they delivered over to all the buffetings of Satan; although they lived only a few rods from the council room. These are some of their names: William Law, one of the first presidency; Wilson Law, brigadier general; Austin Coles, president of the High Council; and Elder Blakesly, who has been the means of bringing upwards of one thousand members into the Church. He has been through nearly all the states in the Union, the Canadas, and England preaching the Gospel. Now look at the great sins they have committed, the Laws' un-Christian-like conduct—Blakesly and others, Apostasy. If it is apostasy to oppose such doctrines and proceedings as I have just mentioned (which are only a few of the enormities taught and practised here), then we hope and pray that all the Church may apostatize.

After they had been thus shamefully treated and published to the world they went and bought a printing press determined to defend themselves against such unhallowed

abuse. It cost them six hundred dollars. [They] commenced
their paper, but Joseph and his clan could not bear the truth
to come out; so after the first number came out Joseph
called his Sanhedrin together; tried the press; condemned it
as a nuisance and ordered the city marshal to take three
hundred armed men and go and burn the press, and if any
offered resistance, to rip them from the guts to the gizzard.
These are his own words. They went and burnt the press,
papers, and household furniture. The Laws, Fosters, Coles,
Hickbies, and others have had to leave the place to save their
lives. Those who have been thus unlawfully cut off have
called a conference; protested against these things; and reorganized the Church. William Law is chosen president; Charles
Ivans, bishop, with the other necessary officers. The Re-
formed Church believe that Joseph has transgressed in his
priestly capacity and has given himself over to serve the
devil, and his own lusts. We will endeavor to send you a
paper and you can then judge for yourselves. They had only
commenced publishing the dark deeds of Nauvoo. A hun-
dredth part has not been told yet.*

The people of the state will not suffer such things any
longer. But I am sorry that the innocent must suffer with the
guilty. I believe there are hundreds of honest hearted souls
in Nauvoo, but none of them I think have forgotten what
they were once taught: that cursed is he that putteth his trust
in man. I would offend some of them more to speak irrev-
erently to Joseph, than it would of God himself. Joseph says
that he is a God to this generation, and I suppose they
believe it. Any one needs a throat like an open sepulchre to
swallow down all that is taught here. There was an elder
once wrote in confidence to a friend in England; told him
the state of the Church here, and they showed it to some of
the elders there, and they wrote back to the heads of the
Church, and it caused him a great deal of trouble. I think if
you would once come here, you would not put so much
confidence in all who go by the name of Mormons.

---

*This letter was written up to this point by Isaac Scott, husband of
Sarah. The rest is in his wife's hand.

I am very much obliged for the pin ball; I think it is very pretty, and it comes from Mother so far, from old Massachusetts. I shall appreciate it highly. My health has been very good since I came to the West notwithstanding it is a sickly part of the country. I enjoy myself well this summer. My husband is every thing I could wish, and I hope we may live all the days of our appointed time together. Joseph had two balls last winter and a dancing-school through the winter. There was a theatre established in the spring; some of the twelve took a part—Erastus Snow and many of the leading members of the Church. Dear Mother, I hope the time is not far distant when we can enjoy each other's society, but when and where I suppose time only will determine. There is a report that a mob is coming to Nauvoo.

Sarah Scott

Evidences
of Plagiarism

❖

We have mentioned before the intertwined lives of Reverend Ethan Smith and Reverend Solomon Spaulding and their common heritage, friendship, and the probable sharing of their views. In this chapter we shall compare Ethan Smith's book, *View of the Hebrews*, with the Book of Mormon. There are hundreds of likenesses between the two books, of which some will be selected. No one has in their possession, that I have knowledge of, the original *Manuscript Found* written by Spaulding. There is great probability that it was destroyed by the Mormon authors after its purpose had been served.

When Ethan Smith published his first copy of the *View of the Hebrews* in 1823 in Poultney, Vermont, Oliver Cowdery was living there. A second printing was done in 1825 and this was the year Cowdery moved to the Palmyra, New York, area. Oliver could have brought a copy of the book with him to New York at that time.

One of the first bits of information which reveals that Joseph had the *View of the Hebrews/Manuscript Found* in hand was in the fall of 1827 when a Reverend John A. Clark of Palmyra tells of a visit he had with Martin Harris. Martin said to Reverend Clark that the "Golden Bible" would be found to contain such disclosures as would speedily bring on the "glorious millennium." Ethan Smith had written in the *View of the Hebrews* that his book was "designed [for] hastening the progress of the Millennial glory." Note that Martin had gotten his information from Joseph Smith.

A Brief Comparative Study between the View of the Hebrews and the Book of Mormon:
(Quotes taken from the Utah edition)

A Hidden Book to be Found

1. Just thirty-seven pages into the Book of Mormon Smith injects a prophecy of "these things shall be hid up to come forth . . ." (I Nephi, 3:185), and then in verse 189, he says, "I beheld other books . . . unto . . . convincing the seed of my brethren."

View of Hebrews—The idea for such a book and its future unveiling: Ethan writes on page 223, ". . . an old Indian informed him that his fathers in this country had not long since had a book which they had for a long time preserved . . ."

Joseph declared that he had found it and that it had been preserved for 1,400 years.

View of Hebrews—Ethan further writes on page 217, "If the Indians are of the Tribe of Israel, some decisive evidence will err long be exhibited . . . Suppose a leading character in Israel . . . should be found to have in his possession some biblical fragment of Ancient Hebrew writing . . . and it is buried with him in such a manner as to be long persevered. Some people afterwards removing the earth, discover the fragment and ascertain what it is."

The Book of Mormon was proclaimed as being the Hebrew writing, the "Stick of Joseph," Smith and company proclaimed early on so as to convey the idea that the Book of Mormon fulfilled Ezekiel the thirty-seventh chapter of the Bible. Smith would also make his discovery by removing a little earth.

Both the *View of the Hebrews* and the Book of Mormon position their leading characters to have their initial vision in the Middle East.

Each Would Make a Journey

2. Both would leave the Jerusalem area.

Both would be traveling to a Promised Land, a land of liberty.

Both would be a broken branch, a remnant of the House of Israel.

Both would be travelling eastward from Jerusalem. Both would proceed to a great Body of Water which stopped their journey for a period of time.

Both would journey to a land, which on page 73 the *View of the Hebrews* says was "unknown to the world as such," and on page 9, the Utah Book of Mormon says that "it was kept from the knowledge of all nations."

Idea of the Olive Tree

3. *View of Hebrews*—made several references to the Olive Tree and Israel being grafted back in. One comparison on page 62 says, "till the fullness of the gentiles be come in and then Israel shall be grafted in again . . . ".

Book of Mormon—pages 22-23, "that after the Gentiles had received the fullness of the Gospel, the natural branches of the Olive Tree, or the remnants of the House of Israel, should be grafted in."

Vision of a Great Nation

4. *View of Hebrews*—page 237, "Casting an eye . . . down to the days of the final restoration of his long rejected brethren . . . a vision to the West . . . to the continent of their long banishment." There the prophet beholds in vision a great nation arising in the last days; a land of freedom.

Book of Mormon—page 26, "The angel said unto me to look, and behold my seed and also the seed of thy brethren! And I looked and beheld the land of promise . . . It shall be a land of liberty." Page 57 goes on to say, "The Lord God will raise up a mighty nation among the Gentiles."

The Bible

5. *View of Hebrews*—page 249, "send them (Indians) the Word, the bread of life, you received that book from the seed of Abraham. All your volume of Salvation was written by the sons of Jacob . . . it was transferred from Jerusalem . . . to you (gentiles)."

Book of Mormon—page 30, "Thou has beheld that the book proceeded forth from the mouth of a Jew . . . go forth from the Jews . . . unto the Gentiles."

Book of Mormon—page 31, "I beheld that it (Bible) came forth from the Gentiles into the . . . (Indians)."

Isles of the Sea

6. Bible—In the King James Version of the Bible, in Isaiah 11, the phrase, "Islands of the sea" is used.

View of Hebrews—page 56, it is modified to " . . . The Lord will set his hand . . . to gather the remnant of his people from the Isles of the sea."

Book of Mormon—pages 51-52, follows the *View of the Hebrews*, " . . . yea, then will he remember the Isles of the sea. . . ."

Four Quarters

7. Bible—Again the King James version in Isaiah 11:12 says, "four corners."

View of Hebrews—page 56, Says "four quarters."

Book of Mormon—pages 51-52, follows suit with "four quarters."

Two Groups—One Idle, the Other Civilized

8. *View of Hebrews*—page 172, says, "Different clans parted from each other, lost each other and formed separate tribes. . . . Most of them fell into a wandering idle hunting life . . . and formed a habit of this idle mode of living, and were pleased with it. More sensible parts of this people associated together, . . . from these the noted relics of civilization discovered in the West and South . . ."

Book of Mormon—The story follows the same line of thought in II Nephi 5:24, "Because of their cursings which was upon them, they did become an idle people, . . . and did seek in the wilderness for the beasts of prey."

Lehi's family would split, forming the Nephites and the Lamanites.

They Became Savage, Wild and Wanderers

9. *View of Hebrews*—pages 172-173, " . . . The greater part of their brethren became savage and wild . . . most of them fell into a wandering idle hunting life."

Book of Mormon—page 144, "They became wild and

ferocious, and a blood thirsty people; feeding upon beasts of prey . . . and wandering about in the wilderness . . ."

Both Desired Death to Their Brethren

10. *View of Hebrews*—page 189, "The savage tribes . . . were intent on destruction of this better part of their brethren."

Book of Mormon—page 145, ". . . and they were continually seeking to destroy us."

Shaven Heads

11. *View of Hebrews*—page 111, shaving their heads—girding of sackcloth.

Book of Mormon—pages 144-145, ". . . short skin girded about their loins, and their heads shaven."

The Idea of Mechanics

12. *View of Hebrews*—page 173, "Mechanic and civil arts . . . ancient works and improvements."

Book of Mormon—page 147, ". . . we . . . became exceedingly rich in gold, . . . silver . . . tin workmanship . . . in machinery . . . iron, copper, brass and steel."

Both Built Temples

13. *View of Hebrews*—page 264, "Who taught the untutored savages to have a Temple of Yohewah; a holy of holies in it . . ."

Pages 116-117 even goes into great detail describing the Temple of Jerusalem.

Book of Mormon—page 72, "I Nephi did construct a Temple; and I did construct it after the manner of the Temple of Solomon . . ."

The Idea of a Great Spirit

14. (This concept was not original with the American Indians.)

View of Hebrews—page 103, here we learn that those far distant savages have ". . . their Great Spirit, who made everything . . ."

Book of Mormon—page 275, "Believest thou that this Great Spirit . . . created all things . . ."

Chosen and Elected People

15. *View of Hebrews*—page 99, "The Indians thus pleased themselves . . . with the idea that God has chosen them from the rest of mankind as his peculiar people."

Book of Mormon—pages 211-312, ". . . we believe thou has separated us from our brethren. We believe that thou has elected . . . and we are a chosen and holy people."

Dry Bones

16.*View of Hebrews*—page 257, "In the vast wilderness of America, a literal wilderness . . . where the dry bones of the outcast of Israel have for thousands of years been scattered."

Book of Mormon—page 200, "And they were lost in the wilderness. Nevertheless, they did find a land which had been peopled; yea, a land which was covered with dry bones . . ."

A Voice Saying Wo-Wo

17.*View of Hebrews*—pages 25-26, "A voice from the east-a voice from the west-a voice from the four winds . . . a voice against the whole people. . . . Wo, wo, to . . . this people!"

Book of Mormon—pages 472-473, "And it came to pass that there was a voice heard among all the inhabitants of the earth upon all the face of this land, crying, Wo, wo, wo, unto this people. . . . Behold, I am Jesus Christ . . ."

Jerusalem

18.*View of Hebrews*—pages 18-19, "O' Jerusalem, Jerusalem: thou that killest the prophets, and stones them that are sent unto thee! How often would I have gathered thy children together, even as a hen gathereth her chickens under her wings; and ye would not! Behold, your house is left unto you desolate . . ."

Book of Mormon—page 472, ". . . ye that dwell at Jerusalem, as ye that have fallen; yea, how oft would I have gathered you as a hen gathereth her chickens, and ye would not . . . O House of Israel, the places of your dwellings shall become desolate."

A Comparison between the Wonders of Nature and the Book of Mormon

(*Wonders of Nature* by Josiah Priest predates Book of Mormon.)

Wonders of Nature—Pages 527-528, "Darkness which may be felt.—Probably this was occasioned by a super abundance of aqueous vapors floating in the atmosphere; which were so thick as to prevent the rays of the sun from penetrating through them; an extraordinary thick mist, supernaturally i.e. miraculously brought on. . . . So deep was the obscurity; and probably such was its nature, that an artificial light could be procured, as the thick clammy vapors would prevent lamps, &c, from burning; or even if they could be ignited, the light, through the palpable obscurity, could diffuse itself to no distance from the burning body . . . [T]he darkness with its attendant horrors lasted for three days . . ."

Book of Mormon—pages 471-472, "And it came to pass that there was thick darkness upon all the face of the land, insomuch that the inhabitants thereof which had not fallen, could feel the vapor of darkness; and there could be no light because of the darkness, neither candles, neither torches; neither could there be fire kindled with their fine and exceeding dry wood, so there could not be any light at all; and there was not any light seen, neither fire, nor glimmer, neither the sun, nor the moon, nor the stars, for so great were the mists of darkness which were upon the face of the land. And it came to pass that it did last for the space of three days that there was no light seen . . ."

The Dream of 1811

When Joseph replaced the 116 pages lost by Martin Harris it sent him digging through his mother's family records and elsewhere. There among his mother's writings he discovered a dream which his father had in 1811. He took this dream and embellished it into a great vision from God and placed it in the first section of the Book of Mormon. This utilization of his father's dream is convicting evidence that Smith drew upon materials at his disposal in the rewriting of the "lost" 116 pages.

The Comparison of His Father's Dream of 1811 and the Vision of Lehi in the Book of Mormon Is as Follows:

Both Were Traveling

Lehi—I Nephi 8:8, "And after I had traveled for the space of many hours . . ."

Joseph—page 58, "'thought,' said he, 'I was t'ravelling. . . .'"

There Was a Field

Lehi—I Nephi 8:4-9 ". . . I saw in my dream, a dark and

dreary wilderness . . . I beheld a large and spacious field."

Joseph—page 58, "'. . . I was traveling in an open, desolate field, which appeared to be very barren.'"

Fields Compared to a World

Lehi—I Nephi 8:20, "And I also behold . . . a large and spacious field, as if it had been a world."

Joseph—page 58, "'. . . an open, desolate field . . . My guide . . . said, this is the desolate world . . .'"

A Guide

Lehi—I Nephi 8:5-6, "And it came to pass that I saw a man, . . . bade me follow him."

Joseph—page 58, "'My guide, who was by my side . . .'"

Broad Road That Leads

Lehi—I Nephi 12:17, ". . . leadeth them away into broad roads, that they perish and are lost."

Joseph—page 58, "'The road was broad and barren . . .'"

Narrow Path

Lehi—I Nephi 8:20, "And I also behold a straight and narrow path, . . ."

Joseph—page 58, "'. . . I came to a narrow path.'"

Stream of Water

Lehi—I Nephi 8:13, ". . . I beheld a river of water . . ."

Joseph—page 58, "'. . . I beheld a beautiful stream of water . . .'"

Each Has an Object along the Bank

Lehi—I Nephi 8:19, "And I beheld a rod of iron, and it extended along the bank of the river . . ."

Joseph—page 58, "'. . . I could see a rope, running along the bank of it . . .'"

There Is a Tree

Lehi—I Nephi 8:10, "And it came to pass that I beheld a tree, . . ."

Joseph—page 58, "'. . . a tree, such as I had never seen . . .'"

Trees Bore Fruit

Lehi—I Nephi 8:10, ". . . whose fruit was desirable to make one happy."

Joseph—page 58, "'. . . it bore a kind of fruit, . . .'"

Fruit White as Snow

Lehi—I Nephi 11:8, ". . . the whiteness thereof did exceed the whiteness of the driven snow."

Joseph—page 58, "'. . . as white as snow, or, if possible, whiter . . .'"

Fruit Is Eaten—Delicious

Lehi—I Nephi 8:11, ". . . it was most sweet, above all that I ever before tasted."

Joseph—page 58, "'. . . and I found it delicious beyond description.'"

Wanted Their Families to Partake

Lehi—I Nephi 8:12, ". . . I began to be desirous that my family should partake of it also; . . ."

Joseph—page 58, "'As I was eating', I said in my heart, 'I cannot eat this alone, I must bring my wife and children, that they may partake with me.'"

Families Partook

Lehi—I Nephi 8:16, ". . . they did come unto me and partake of the fruit also."

Joseph—page 58, "'. . . I went and brought my family, . . . and we all commenced eating . . .'"

All Experienced Great Joy

Lehi—I Nephi 8:12, ". . . it filled my soul with exceeding great joy; . . ."

Joseph—pages 58-59, "'. . . exceedingly happy, insomuch that our joy could not easily be expressed.'"

Each Beheld a Spacious Building

Lehi—I Nephi 8:26, ". . . A great and spacious building; . . ."

Joseph—page 59, "'. . . I beheld a spacious building . . .'"

Building Extremely High

Lehi—I Nephi 8:26, ". . . it stood as it were in the air, high above the earth."

Joseph—page 59, "'. . . it appeared to reach to the very heavens.'"

Filled with People

Lehi—I Nephi 8:27, "And it was filled with people, . . ."

Joseph—page 59, "'. . . they were all filled with people . . .'"

Finely Dressed

Lehi—I Nephi 8:27, ". . . their manner of dress was exceeding fine; . . ."

Joseph—page 59, "'. . . who were finely dressed.'"

Finger of Scorn

Lehi—I Nephi 8:33, ". . . they did point the finger of scorn at me . . ."

Joseph—page 59, "'. . . they pointed the finger of scorn at us, . . .'"

Ignored the Scorn

Lehi—I Nephi 8:33, ". . . but we heeded them not."

Joseph—page 59, "'. . . we utterly disregarded.'"

Describes Fruit as Pure Love of God

Lehi—I Nephi 11:21-22, ". . . the meaning of the tree which thy father saw? And I answered him, saying: Yea, it is the love of God, . . ."

Joseph—page 59, "'I . . . inquired . . . the meaning of the fruit . . . He told me it was the pure love of God, . . .'"

Families Missing Two Members

Lehi—I Nephi 8:17, ". . . I was desirous that Laman and Lemuel should come and partake of the fruit . . ."

Joseph—page 59, "'. . . you have two more, and you must bring them also.'"

Each Building Falls

Lehi—I Nephi 11:36, ". . . spacious building . . . fell . . ."

Joseph—page 59, "'. . . the meaning of the spacious building which I saw.' He replied, 'It is Babylon, . . . it must fall.'"

Both Imply Pride

Lehi—I Nephi 11:36, ". . . the great and spacious building was the pride of the world; . . ."

Joseph—page 59, "'The people in the doors and windows are the inhabitants thereof, who scorn and despise the Saints of God because of their humility'" (Jerald and Sandra Tanner, *Mormonism—Shadow Or Reality*, Salt Lake City, Utah, pp. 86-87).

The evidences of plagiarism as shown in this chapter are but a small fraction of the vast amount of borrowing which was done to create the Book of Mormon. The Bible was very extensively drawn upon as the Book of Mormon was formed.

The Book of Mormon is nothing more than a conglomeration of many writings, of which the work of Solomon

Spaulding was only one, although it was perhaps the skeleton upon which the body was formed.

CHAPTER NINETEEN

Universalism with New Age Overtones

❖

Perhaps no evidence anywhere is more supportive to Sidney Ridgon's authorship of the theology found in the Book of Mormon, than to learn that Joseph, Sr., and Joseph, Jr., were both Universalists in their theology. Joseph Smith, Sr., was a member of a universalist society while living in Vermont (M & Mager p. 90). What is taught in the Book of Mormon is fundamental Bible Christianity with strong emphasis on the popular "Disciples of Christ" doctrines which Rigdon had been preaching. Joseph, Jr., was not raised amidst a solid biblical doctrinal background. It was neither in his faith nor his household. It is true that the Bible was drawn upon hundreds of times in the formation of the Book of Mormon, but this again leans toward Rigdon, Ethan, and Spaulding as students of the scriptures.

The following excerpts from the Book of Mormon could no more have come from the mind and soul of Joseph Smith in 1829 than a pine tree could have come from an acorn.

> I glory in plainness, I glory in truth, I glory in my Jesus, for he hath redeemed my soul from hell . . . But behold for none of these can I hope, except they shall be reconciled unto Christ, and enter into the straight gate, and walk in the straight path, which leads to life and con-

tinue in the path until the end of the Day of Probation.
(RLDS Book of Mormon, II Nephi, p. 165)

Again,

Therefore, if that man repenteth not and dieth an en-
emy to God, the demands of justice doth awaken his
immortal soul to a lively sense of his own guilt, which
cause him; to shrink from the presence of the Lord, and
doth fill his breast with guilt, and pain, and anguish,
which is like an unquenchable fire whose flames ascended
up forever and ever. And now I say unto you, that mercy
hath no claim on that man; therefore, his final doom is
to endure a never ending torment. (RLDS Book of Mormon, Mosiah, p. 215)

Joseph Smith could not have conceived the above. This
teaching was foreign to his up bringing. His father believed
that all men would eventually be saved, a doctrine having
imbedded itself in America from a Dr. George de Benneville
(1709-1793). The promise of Universal Christianity is that all
men would finally be redeemed by the love of God (Harry
Cheetham, *Unitarian and Universalism*, 1962, p. 75).

One year after Smith and Rigdon moved the Mormon
Church to Kirtland, Ohio, Joseph Smith's true doctrine sur-
faced in a revelation given to him and Rigdon in a vision.
This revelation is dated 16 February 1832. A portion of it
reads,

And thus we saw in the heavenly vision, the glory of the
telestial some of the inhabitants of this Kingdom glory are
. . . These are they who are liars and sorcerers, and adulter-
ers, and whoremongers whosoever loves and makes a lie. .
. . These are they who are cast down to hell and suffer the
wrath of God until the fullness of times. . . . (RLDS D&C,
Sec. 76)

Then at the end of the millennium they come forth to
receive the telestial eternal heavenly glory. In Mormon theology there are three Kingdoms of Glory of which the telestial
is the third in rank. This revelation confirms two things: one,
that Joseph Smith was a Universalist in his beliefs; and second, his ability to call up spirit manifestations to assist him
in the establishing of his doctrines. This experience was so

powerful that it swayed Rigdon from his Bible position. Surely Rigdon knew that such a doctrine directly contradicted both the Bible and his Book of Mormon. It took Joseph Smith only eighteen months to break with main line Christianity on its most vital doctrine, the doctrine of salvation. Smith also lost some of his followers over this revelation. Those that left the church told him the revelation was of the devil!

To illustrate the effect such revelations have had on some of Smith's priesthood I share the following: Approximately nineteen years ago (1974), I was in conversation with an RLDS Mormon elder in Independence, Missouri. He stated very forthrightly that he believed that the day would come when Satan and his angels would again be gathered back into the Kingdom of God.

False doctrine will always beget false doctrine in one form or another. When false spirits are operating in a church or its priesthood, that church will always be unsettled in its doctrine. This has been true of Mormonism as these deceiving spirits have led them in many diverse directions. The RLDS has been led, in the last forty years, off into liberalism and have gone awhoring into the Babylonian religious philosophy of the "New Age" movement, while still operating under the thin cover that they are still followers of the revelations of Joseph Smith.

A New Age Temple?

Recently the RLDS have completed a very elaborate temple in Independence, Missouri. For justifying the spending of this kind of money for one building, the Mormon leadership used a revelation given by Joseph Smith in 1831. Smith declared by revelation that the Lord said a temple was to be built in Independence. But Smith had a stipulation in his revelation which declared that the temple was to be reared in his generation. Smith could not fulfill his prophecy there in Independence because he and his followers were chased from Missouri back into Illinois. It was there in Illinois where Smith apparently fulfilled his prophecy, by constructing a temple in his city of Nauvoo.

In keeping with the spirit of the original Mormon prophet,

approximately fifty million dollars was spent by the Missouri
Mormons to construct an edifice whose image reflects the
spirit of the New Age movement. This temple carries in its
design a close resemblance to the ancient ziggurrat of
Babylon. Since the New Age movement of today carries
within its doctrines very strong influences from the old
Babylonian religion, then it should not be surprising that
these Mormons were led to construct their temple in the
likeness of the old Babylonian ziggurrat. According to their
present prophet, Smith, a great-grandson of Joseph, Jr., the
Mormon Temple will be a place where all religions can
gather for dialogue.

The temple itself has been dedicated to world peace,
which is one of the leading objectives of the New Age movement. It will be interesting to observe the strategy these
Mormons will seek to follow in the coming days. The Mormons have held dear in their teaching that when the temple
was built, it would signal that God's appointed time had
come to bestow upon all who were worthy through certain
temple rites a great endowment of His Spirit.

We find among the New Age believers a similar teaching, where there is to be given to all who are properly
prepared a special endowment of light. This glorious manifestation is described by some prominent New Age writers
as the receiving of the "Third Eye." The "Third Eye" is a
demon spirit which takes up residence at the front of the
brain just behind the center of the forehead. From this
position it can monitor all the conscious thoughts of the
individual. This demon's role will play a very important part
of assisting Satan in maintaining worldwide control. The
power of the "Third Eye" appears to be the spiritual mark
which Satan plans to anoint millions of the earth's inhabitants with in his effort to bring about his system of world
peace. The Bible says, "Woe to the inhabiters of the earth
and of the sea! for the devil is come down unto you, having
great wrath, because he knoweth that he hath but a short
time" (Revelations 12:12).

We have in recent years begun to get a glimpse of the
great numbers of perverted, lying, and deceiving spirits which
Satan is unleashing throughout the world. This new world

order of peace, which both Bush and Clinton are committed to, will soon be preached not just by the TV commentators, but will be heard expounded in many of the pulpits across the land. We will soon be hearing a gospel of peace and unity, proclaiming that our world can only become safe as we join together as one big family; where we all will be asked to work together for the common good of humanity; where we shall all be required to abide by laws which will be enacted for the common welfare for the world at large. This grand movement of peace will be designed to touch and control every detail of a person's life. To this monster we shall all become its slave.

What does the Bible have to say about this kind of peace? Jesus said, "Peace I leave with you, my peace I give unto you: not as the world giveth, give I unto you" (John 14:27a).

This Mormon Temple has been set apart where the religions of this earth can gather for dialogue. Dialogue means to exchange ideas and opinions. Jesus is not offering nor considering dialogue with the world in this statement. What He is implying is that His peace has no resemblance to that of the world. Speaking of peace He said,

> Think not that I am come to send peace on earth: I came not to send peace, but a sword. For I am come to set a man at variance against his father, and the daughter against her mother, and the daughter in law against her mother in law. And a man's foes shall be they of his own household. (Matthew 10:34-36)

Jesus further declared, "My Kingdom is not of this world . . ." (John 18:36).

I personally cannot fathom that any born-again follower of Jesus could even for a moment think of sitting down with professors representing demonically inspired and controlled religions for an exchange of ideas and opinions. The Apostle Paul admonished us with these words, "Be ye not unequally yoked together with unbelievers: for what fellowship hath righteousness with unrighteousness? *and what communion hath light with darkness?* And what concord hath Christ with Be'lial? or what part hath he that believeth with an infidel?" (emphasis mine, II Corinthians 6:14-15).

Such intentions by these Mormons certainly causes one to suspect that to them, Jesus is not The Way, The Truth, and The Life, and that his name is not the only name given under heaven whereby man can be saved. The Bible has foretold that the day would come when men would permit themselves to be deceived. It reads, "And many false prophets shall rise, and shall deceive many" (Matthew 24:11–KJV).

To imply, as these Mormons have done, that the Gospel of Jesus Christ can be placed upon the altar of compromise is fostering a deception of the worst kind. The apostle prophesied of that end-time peace effort: "For yourselves know perfectly that the day of the Lord so cometh as a thief in the night. For when they shall say, peace and safety; then sudden destruction cometh upon them, as travail upon a woman with child; and they shall not escape" (I Thessalonians 5:2-3).

This great concern over world peace has continued to intensify, and now voices can be heard saying that peace must come regardless of the price. There is no cost too great to be made. But before such an objective will be able to make much headway, certain planned events will transpire which will persuade the masses that such a compromise is the only answer if life on this planet is to be stabilized. In this philosophy nothing is too sacred which cannot be sacrificed upon the "altar of peace."

In light of this cry for world peace the new Mormon temple could be prophetic after all, in that its dedication to world peace could be taken as a warning sign trumpeting the soon-coming destruction as prophesied by the Apostle Paul.

How interesting indeed, that the first Mormon prophet, Joseph Smith, Jr., is playing such a vital role in this great end-time deception of world peace. The temple which they have constructed has been a Mormon dream for over 160 years. This dream was born from revelation given by Smith in 1831 in Jackson County, Independence, Missouri, while he was standing just a few yards from the present temple.

The end-time peace will require a joint effort of all religions. Sweeping compromises will be expedient upon most, if not all, before such a peace can be obtained. But there is no question that the greatest compromise will come from the Christian faith for the sake of "world peace." Many Christians will not only trample upon the "Blood of Jesus" and pollute its most essential truths, but will simultaneously embrace the apostate doctrine of the Antichrist.

The social pressure, as well as the popularity of such a compromise, will release an overpowering temptation to join its ranks. The message of it all will ring as if it were the voice of John the Baptist crying as it were to prepare the way for the coming of the Lord. This unification will appear so right to the natural mind that only a "fool" would reject the "wondrous" blessing it will bring to all the earth.

Already we see Pope John Paul II preparing the minds of the Catholics for this New Age compromise. He is preaching that there are many paths to God. He has fellowshipped with witch doctors, gurus, and most recently hosted the Dalai Lama of Tibetan Buddhism. The Associated Press released the following from Cotonou, Benin (Africa): "Pope John II on Thursday sought common ground with the believers in voodoo, suggesting they would not betray their traditional faith by converting to Christianity."

Vast millions will feed upon such propaganda as being preached by the pope and blindly be led into the "lie of the ages." The Apostle John, by the spirit of prophecy, warned the people of God of our day and time. "Because thou has kept the word of my patience, I also will keep thee from the hour of temptation, which shall come upon all the world, to try them that dwell upon the earth. Behold, I come quickly: hold that fast which thou hast, that no man take thy crown" (Revelations 3:10-11—KJV).

Several years ago before the present RLDS Mormon leader, Mr. Wallace B. Smith, had assumed his position as leader of that faction of Mormonism, I had an interesting dream about him. I had never met him prior to the dream. I was introduced to him several years later after he had assumed his present position as president of the RLDS Church by Dr. Roy Cheville, who was once the presiding patriarch of the RLDS Church. The dream occurred in 1968 while my family and I were still living in the state of California. In the dream a meeting was being held in an old school house out in the country. I was aware in the dream that it was not too far from Independence, Missouri. Everyone in the room was acutely aware of the extreme state of tribulation we were all presently passing through. The attitude of mind was a very sober one for all who were present.

Mr. Smith was seated to my extreme left on the front row. In the dream I knew who he was and the position he held. I knew from that experience that he would eventually become the leader of the RLDS Mormons. I was occupying the pulpit and was speaking relative to the prevailing conditions.

But what has remained with me all these years is the great attentiveness Mr. Smith was giving to what was being said. The expression on his face revealed that he was hearing words which, if heeded, would determine whether or not one would survive the terrible ordeal that had come upon the earth. In the dream he listened to every word with deep sincerity. The only other thing of significance that happened was that a hunchback man slipped across the rear of the room and up to the side where Mr. Smith was sitting. The man whispered something to him. Mr. Smith refused to be distracted and turned to the man and bid him go. I knew that the man represented a "lying spirit."

I believe this experience implied that as the conditions in the world continue to deteriorate, Mr. Smith would take a firm stand with the Son of God and reject the coming ungodly compromise. If he does this, as the dream indicated, his followers will be few. He will suffer that which Jesus did, where many will turn and will follow him no more. He will be viewed by many of his followers as being out of step with the times. It is very possible that he would be asked to step down by the powers who surround him.

Before this great world religious compromise occurs, ways of escape will be prepared for the pure in heart and for those who truly desire for Jesus to be their only Lord. I believe that many Mormons will be spared this great end time deception as they turn to trust Jesus and look to Him as the only true Shepherd, and realizing that His Word alone is the only saving Word of Truth. Mormonism was a cunningly devised fable; a fable which was birthed in deception and darkness. According to the Apostle Paul, there can be no communion between "light and darkness." But when one is willing to compromise the Word of God with the fables of men and doctrines of devils, he is seeking to do the impossible. He will not be successful in the eyes of God. Rather he will be known as "a foolish man who built his house upon the sand" (Matthew 7:26). But to those who would believe His Word, Jesus warned, "For as a snare shall it come on all them that dwell on the face of the whole earth. Watch ye therefore, and pray always, that ye may be accounted worthy to escape all these things that shall come to pass and to stand before the Son of man" (Luke 21:35, 36).

CHAPTER TWENTY

No Other Name Given under Heaven—(Acts 4:12)

❖

As a Mormon I was baptized at the appropriate age of eight, being obedient to the Mormon doctrine and believing with all my heart that I was joining the only true and living church of the Lord. I felt at the time surely this was enough to save me. In my heart I had joined the Lord's Church. Shortly thereafter, hands were laid upon my head for the Baptism of the Holy Ghost, and I went from the meeting that day, feeling I had done what was expected. Now that I was a member they could not pass me by with the bread and wine.

My life in Mormonism stayed pretty much in the same mold and spirit for the next fourteen years. At this period of time I was now in the army, stationed at Fort Jackson, South Carolina. There I met a young man, and as our friendship began to grow, I desired greatly to make a Mormon out of him. Let me say at this juncture, most Mormons will try to convert you. They have that feeling down inside that will never be content until non-Mormons come to accept their church, their doctrines, and their god.

I set out to proselytize the young man. He was responding real well and was reading some material I had given him. I was very diligent in exalting Joseph Smith as God's special prophet and all about the coming forth of the true church.

One morning, a few minutes before the summoning of the
wake up call, I had a dream concerning this young man and
myself walking on the base. We were headed to the dairy
freeze. He was on my right side, and I remember as we
walked along that we both were enjoying the time together.
It was getting late and the sun was beginning to set in the
west. I looked across at the sun and was thinking how large
and orange it was, when suddenly the face of Jesus appeared
in the sun. Jesus looked straight into my eyes and the moment my eye caught His, He faded from the sun. Every time
I would look back at the sun after that there He was looking
at me. Instantly I awoke, and rolled to the side of the bunk
with the picture of Jesus branded into my mind. For the next
few weeks I needed only to close my eyes to relive that face
looking at me. Nine more years would pass before I really
would understand the meaning of that experience that
morning in South Carolina.

I went to church, said my prayers, read the Bible, Book
of Mormon, and *Doctrine and Covenants*. I didn't smoke,
drink, swear, or so forth. I was a good Mormon. But I didn't
understand what the Apostle Paul wrote, "My righteousness
was as filthy rags." I was blinded by my religious experience
to the truth of this. I could not relate to the gospel song
which says, "Once I was blind, but now I see."

In 1964 we had moved to southern California; there I
became good friends with a Full Gospel minister who taught
in the same school with me. One day he asked me a question; he said, "Barney, can you say that you have received the
Baptism of the Holy Ghost?" At the time of the question I
had a major in religion, was an ordained Mormon elder and
had spent a lot of time in study. But at that moment I could
not give him a satisfactory answer to the question, which for
some reason both offended and embarrassed me at the same
time. In the midst of my great Mormon pride I turned to
him (His name was Emmanuel—interesting name.) and finally said, "I can't really say that I have received the Baptism
of the Holy Ghost." I remember walking away from him that
day, pridefully hurt, but saying to myself, "I am going to find
out if there is a Holy Ghost." I surely didn't know the Holy
Ghost and I didn't know the Lord either. All I knew was a

religion and a church! This marked the first time in which I would in sincerity reach out to God for the purpose of knowing Him.

I had prayed to the Lord many times, but had never personally desired to seek Him with all my heart. The apostle wrote that God isn't very far from any of us if we would but make some attempt to feel after him. "Whom to know," Paul said, "is life eternal." To the Phillipian saints he wrote, ". . . I count all things but loss for the excellency of the knowledge of Christ Jesus my Lord: for whom I have suffered the loss of all things, and do count them but dung, that I may win Christ, And be found in Him, not having my own righteousness . . . but that which is through the faith of Christ, the righteousness which is of God by faith" (Philippians 3:8-9). Never in all the years of reading the above had the apostle's words ever come alive to me.

As the days passed, my desiring for the Baptism of the Holy Spirit began to create a deeper hunger within to know the Lord. One evening, as I had finished praying and was just saying, "Thank you Jesus" very personably to the Lord, His Spirit came upon me and He spoke these words, "I am mighty to save." I hadn't given any thought to the fact that I needed to be saved. I had joined what I believed to be His Church, but apparently I had missed something. After He spoke, He lifted His Spirit. I still did not know exactly what to do. But the Lord was merciful and very shortly thereafter I was at a meeting in Glendale, California, and was introduced to the Lord and led in a simple prayer, where I asked Jesus to come into my heart.

Some preachers will tell you that it is too childish—it's too simple. No, it isn't simple when you are filled with religious pride, like I was. It took a melting process within before I could look up and in faith ask the Lord to come into my heart.

When Jesus comes into your heart things are different. No one can add to the things which He brings. Jesus said, "Behold I stand at the door and knock: and if any man hear my voice, and open the door, I will come in to him, and will sup with him, and he with me" (Revelations 3:20—KJV).

No religion, *no* church, no other person can open that

door, only you and I. We must by faith, from a desire deep within and by the words of our mouth, say out loud, "Lord Jesus come into my heart, I do want to sup with You!" "I do want to know You!" "I do want you above all else to be my Lord!" The Apostle Paul wrote, ". . . if thou shalt confess with thy mouth the Lord Jesus, and shalt believe in thine heart that God hath raised him from the dead, thou shalt be saved. For with the heart man believeth unto righteousness; and with the mouth confession is made unto salvation" (Romans 10:9-10–KJV).

Shortly after receiving Jesus came the Baptism in the Holy Ghost, the effect of which spread to my wife, and soon the joy of the Lord filled our house.

The night that my wife, Joanne, was born–again and filled with the Baptism of the Holy Ghost she had a vision of Jesus dying for her upon the Cross. That night God revealed to her what the sins of this world had cost Him. Through it all she was taught of God's great love for her and for all men. That love was made real as she witnessed the suffering and the shame He endured upon the Cross.

I shall never forget the affect that Jesus had upon our little daughter, Robin, who was only three-years-old at the time. Every night I had to tell her stories of Jesus. Then one night when I tucked her into bed, she looked up at me with an expression I had never seen before, and said, "Daddy can I see Jesus?" Her eyes never flinched, they fastened upon mine for an answer, and finally I said, "Yes, honey you can see Jesus, I'll kneel down and ask Him to come and visit you." I never thought about the prayer again, until I returned from school one day and she was standing at the screen door waiting for me. As I went into the house, she took me by the hand and said, "Daddy I want to take you into my bedroom, I have something to show you." She took me into her bedroom and walked over to a certain place on the bed and put her hand there and patted the bed. Looking at me she said, "Daddy, Jesus came to see me last night and this is where He sat. He lifted me up and held me in his lap, talked to me and let me feel His beard."

It would take a book to tell all that has happened since those days, twenty-six years ago, in Southern California. Yes, the Lord is precious, wonderful, and so very good to those who call upon His Name. Yes, He is mighty to save!

Jesus is not far from any of us. The truth of the gospel has not changed. "Whosoever will call upon the Name of the Lord shall be saved." Religions have sent men in all directions. Their doctrines, as well as their philosophies, have brought only darkness into the minds of those who followed. How vain we have been in our attempts to sup from the cups of men and demons. When all along Jesus is waiting and knocking, intensely yearning for us to personally become intimate friends with Him. We read of that intimacy of which Jesus speaks in John 6:53, ". . . Verily, verily, I say unto you, Except ye eat the flesh of the Son of man, and drink his blood, ye have no life in you."

During this century the spiritual understanding of how an individual can experience the power which resides in both the Blood and the Word of the Lord has greatly waned. Most of the Christian world has lost its true focus of faith. The understanding of this focus is made very clear by the Apostle Paul in his writings to the Hebrews: "Wherefore seeing we also are compassed about with so great a cloud of witnesses, let us lay aside every weight, and the sin which doth so easily beset us, and let us run with patience the race that is set before us, Looking unto Jesus the author and finisher of our faith; who for the joy that was set before him endured the cross, despising the shame, and is set down at the right hand of the throne of God" (Hebrews 12:1-2). Jesus alone is the One upon whom the faith of our soul must rest.

Life in this world, apart from His continual care, is filled with the worst forms of deceptive selfishness, fear, and death. The pressures and temptations which are bearing down upon every individual are too great for the scripturally weak to overcome. Today, the mad rush toward material riches and success is tearing millions of lives and families to shreds, leaving many wounded and lost along its destructive pathway of darkness.

Jesus not only desires to save us from this blinding curse

of selfishness, but to deliver us from religious spirits which feed our ego and blinds us from the simplicity that is in Him. He is always so willing to prepare before us a table in the presence of these ever deceiving enemies of our soul. Jesus knows far better than any how desperately every person needs Him in their life.

Today, as we are living in the very last days, before the Lord shall come, the Bible tells us that iniquity will wax worse and worse and false religions and prophets will arise all over the world. Satan, knowing his time is short, is turning loose everything in his arsenal to deceive even the "very elect." A hypocritical, compromising, watered-down faith in Jesus will not get one through in this hour. The pressure to rewrite the precious Word of God to this world's corrupted standards is being heard everywhere. John the apostle, seeing our day, warned us with these words: "And I heard another voice from heaven, saying, Come out of her, my people, that ye be not partakers of her sins, and that ye receive not of her plagues" (Revelation 18:4—KJV).

But to the faithful, to the obedient, and to those who love not their lives even unto death, he wrote, "He that overcometh, the same shall be clothed in white raiment; and I will not blot his name out of the book of life, but I will confess his name before my Father, and before his angels" (Revelations 3:5—KJV).

Perhaps the purest sermon ever preached under the anointing of the Holy Ghost concerning Jesus, since the Christian age began, was preached by the Apostle Peter shortly after Pentecost. No Scripture has been of more value to those who have believed its Word than this which Peter proclaimed that day "Neither is there salvation in any other: for there is none other name under heaven given among men, whereby we must be saved" (Acts 4:12—KJV).

More Good Books From
HUNTINGTON HOUSE PUBLISHERS

RECENT RELEASES

Gays & Guns
The Case against Homosexuals in the Military
by John Eidsmoe

The homosexual revolution seeks to overthrow the Laws of Nature. A Lieutenant Colonel in the United States Air Force Reserve, Dr. John Eidsmoe eloquently contends that admitting gays into the military would weaken the combat effectiveness of our armed forces. This cataclysmic step would also legitimize homosexuality, a lifestyle that most Americans know is wrong.

While echoing Cicero's assertion that "a sense of what is right is common to all mankind," Eidsmoe rationally defends his belief. There are laws that govern the universe, he reminds us. Laws that compel the earth to rotate on its axis, laws that govern the economy; and so there is also a moral law that governs man's nature. The violation of this moral law is physically, emotionally and spiritually destructive. It is destructive to both the individual and to the community of which he is a member.

ISBN Trade Paper 1-56384-043-X $7.99

ISBN Hardcover 1-56384-046-4 $14.99

Trojan Horse—
How the New Age Movement Infiltrates the Church
by Samantha Smith & Brenda Scott

New Age/Occult concepts and techniques are being introduced into all major denominations. The revolution is subtle, cumulative, and deadly. Through what door has this heresy entered the church? Authors Samantha Smith and Brenda Scott attempt to demonstrate that Madeleine L'Engle has been and continues to be a major New Age source of entry into the church. Because of her radical departure from traditional Christian theology, Madeleine L'Engle's writings have sparked a wave of controversy across the nation. She has been published and promoted by numerous magazines, including *Today's Christian Woman, Christianity Today* and others. The deception, unfortunately, has been so successful that otherwise discerning congregations and pastors have fallen into the snare that has been laid.

Sadly, many Christians are embracing the demonic doctrines of the New Age movement. Well hidden under "Christian" labels, occult practices, such as Zen meditation, altered states, divinations, out of body experences, "discovering the Divine truth within" and others have defiled many. This book explores the depths of infiltration and discusses ways to combat it.

ISBN 1-56384-040-5 $9.99

A Jewish Conservative Looks at Pagan America
by Don Feder

With eloquence and insight that rival contemporary commentators and essayists of antiquity, Don Feder's pen finds his targets in the enemies of God, family, and American tradition and morality. Deftly ... delightfully ... the master allegorist and Titian with a typewriter brings clarity to the most complex sociological issues and invokes giggles and wry smiles from both followers and foes. Feder is Jewish to the core, and he finds in his Judaism no inconsistency with an American Judeo-Christian ethic. Questions of morality plague school administrators, district court judges, senators, congressmen, parents, and employers; they are wrestling for answers in a "changing world." Feder challenges this generation and directs inquirers to the original books of wisdom: the Torah and the Bible.

ISBN 1-56384-036-7 Trade Paper $9.99

ISBN 1-56384-037-5 Hardcover $19.99

Don't Touch That Dial: The Impact of the Media on Children and the Family
by Barbara Hattemer & Robert Showers

Men and women without any stake in the outcome of the war between the pornographers and our families have come to the qualified, professional agreement that media does have an effect on our children—an effect that is devastatingly significant. Highly respected researchers, psychologists, and sociologists join a bevy of pediatricians, district attorneys, parents, teachers, pastors, and community leaders—who have diligently remained true to the fight against pornographic media—in their latest comprehensive critique of the modern media establishment (i.e., film, television, print, art, curriculum).

ISBN 1-56384-032-4 Trade Paper $9.99

ISBN 1-56384-035-9 Hardcover $19.99

Political Correctness: The Cloning of the American Mind
by David Thibodaux, Ph.D.

The author, a professor of literature at the University of Southwestern Louisiana, confronts head on the movement that is now being called Political Correctness. Political correctness, says Thibodaux, "is an umbrella under which advocates of civil rights, gay and lesbian rights, feminism, and environmental causes have gathered." To incur the wrath of these groups, one only has to disagree with them on political, moral, or social issues. To express traditionally Western concepts in universities today can result in not only ostracism, but even suspension. (According to a recent "McNeil-Lehrer News Hour" report, one student was suspended for discussing the reality of the moral law with an avowed homosexual. He was reinstated only after he apologized.)

ISBN 1-56384-026-X Trade Paper $9.99

Subtle Serpent: New Age in the Classroom
by Darylann Whitemarsh & Bill Reisman

There is a new morality being taught to our children in public schools. Without the consent or even awareness of parents—educators and social engineers are aggressively introducing new moral codes to our children. In most instances, these new moral codes contradict traditional values. Darylann Whitemarsh (a 1989 Teacher of the Year recipient) and Bill Reisman (educator and expert on the occult) combine their knowledge to expose the deliberate madness occurring in our public schools.

ISBN 1-56384-016-2 $9.99

When the Wicked Seize a City
by Chuck & Donna McIlhenny with Frank York

A highly publicized lawsuit . . . a house fire-bombed in the night . . . the shatter of windows smashed by politically (and wickedly) motivated vandals cuts into the night. . . . All this because Chuck McIlhenny voiced God's condemnation of a behavior and life-style and protested the destruction of society that results from its practice. That behavior is homosexuality, and that life-style is the gay culture. This book explores: the rise of gay power and what it will mean if Christians do not organize and prepare for the battle.

ISBN 1-56384-024-3 $9.99

Loyal Opposition:
A Christian Response to the Clinton Agenda
by John Edismoe

The night before the November 1992 elections, a well-known evangelist claims to have had a dream. In this dream, he says, God told him that Bill Clinton would be elected President, and Christians should support his Presidency. What are we to make of this? Does it follow that, because God allowed Clinton to be President; therefore, God wants Clinton to be president? Does God want everything that God allows? Is it possible for an event to occur even though that event displeases God? How do we stand firm in our opposition to the administration's proposals when those proposals contradict Biblical values? And how do we organize and work effectively for constructive action to restore our nation to basic values?

ISBN 1-56384-044-8 $8.99

I Shot and Elephant in My Pajamas—The Morrie Ryskind Story
by Morrie Ryskind with John H. M. Roberts

The Morrie Ryskind story is a classic American success story. The son of Russian Jewish immigrants, Ryskind went on to attend Columbia University and achieve legendary fame on Broadway and in Hollywood, win the Pulitzer Prize, and become a noted nationally syndicated columnist. Writing with his legendary theatrical collabora-tors George S. Kaufman and George and Ira Gershwin, their political satires had an enormous impact on the development of the musical comedy. In Hollywood, many classic films and four of the Marx Brothers' sublime romps—also bear the signatory stamp of genius—Morrie Ryskind.

Forced by his increasingly conservative views to abandon script-writing in Hollywood, Ryskind had the satisifcation near the end of his life to welcome into his home his old friend, the newly elected Presdent of the United States, Ronald Reagan.

In 1983, at the age of 89, Morrie Ryskind finally heeded the pleas of many friends and began work on his autobiography, workng in collaboration with John H. M. Roberts. *I Shot an Elephant in My Pajamas* is the result. You will find that this too-long delayed book was well worth the wait.

ISBN 1-56384-000-6 $12.99

Backlist/Best-sellers

Deadly Deception
by Jim Shaw & Tom McKenney

For the first time the 33 degree ritual is made public! Learn of the "secrets" and "deceptions" that are practiced daily around the world. Find out why Freemasonry teaches that it is the true religion, that all other religions are only corrupted and perverted forms of Freemasonry. If you know anyone in the Masonic movement, you must read this book.

ISBN 0-910311-54-4 $8.99

Exposing the AIDS Scandal
by Dr. Paul Cameron

Where do you turn when those who control the flow of information in this country withhold the truth? Why is the national media hiding facts from the public? Can AIDS be spread in ways we're not being told? Finally, a book that gives you a total account for the AIDS epidemic, and what steps can be taken to protect yourself. What you don't know can kill you!

ISBN 0-910311-52-8 $7.99

Hidden Dangers of the Rainbow
by Constance Cumbey

The first book to uncover and expose the New Age movement, this national #1 best-seller paved the way for all other books on the subject. It has become a giant in its category. This book provides the vivid expose of the New Age movement, which the author contends is dedicated to wiping out Christianity and establishing a one world order. This movement, a vast network of occult and pagan organizations, meets the tests of prophecy concerning the Antichrist.

ISBN 0-910311-03-X $9.99

Kinsey, Sex and Fraud:
The Indoctrination of a People
by Dr. Judith A. Reisman and Edward Eichel

Kinsey, Sex and Fraud describes the research of Alfred Kinsey which shaped Western society's beliefs and understanding of the nature of human sexuality. His unchallenged conclusions are taught at every level of education—elementary, high school and college—and quoted in textbooks as undisputed truth.

The authors clearly demonstrate that Kinsey's research involved illegal experimentations on several hundred children. The survey was carried out on a non-representative group of Americans, including disproportionately large numbers of sex offenders, prostitutes, prison inmates and exhibitionists.

ISBN 0-910311-20-X $10.99

"Soft Porn" Plays Hardball
by Dr. Judith A. Reisman

With amazing clarity, the author demonstrates that pornography imposes on society a view of women and children that encourages violence and sexual abuse. As crimes against women and children increase to alarming proportions, it's of paramount importance that we recognize the cause of this violence. Pornography should be held accountable for the havoc it has wreaked in our homes and our country.

ISBN 0-910311-65-X Trade Paper $8.99
ISBN 0-910311-92-7 Hardcover $16.95

ORDER THESE HUNTINGTON HOUSE BOOKS !

_____	America Betrayed—Marlin Maddoux	$6.99 _____
_____	Angel Vision (A Novel)—Jim Carroll with Jay Gaines	5.99 _____
_____	Battle Plan: Equipping the Church for the 90s—Chris Stanton	7.99 _____
_____	Blessings of Liberty—Charles C. Heath	8.99 _____
_____	*Christ Returns to the Soviets—Greg Gulley/Kim Parker	9.99 _____
_____	Deadly Deception: Freemasonry—Tom McKenney	8.99 _____
_____	The Delicate Balance—John Zajac	8.99 _____
_____	Dinosaurs and the Bible—Dave Unfred	12.99 _____
_____	*Don't Touch That Dial—Barbara Hattemer & Robert Showers	9.99/19.99 _____
_____	En Route to Global Occupation—Gary Kah	9.99 _____
_____	Exposing the AIDS Scandal—Dr. Paul Cameron	7.99 _____
_____	Face the Wind—Gloria Delaney	9.99 _____
_____	False Security—Jerry Parks	9.99 _____
_____	From Rock to Rock—Eric Barger	8.99 _____
_____	*Gays & Guns—John Eidsmoe	7.99/14.99 _____
_____	*A Generation Betrayed—Randy Kirk	9.99 _____
_____	*Heresy Hunters—Jim Spencer	9.99 _____
_____	Hidden Dangers of the Rainbow—Constance Cumbey	9.99 _____
_____	*Hitler and the New Age—Bob Rosio	9.99 _____
_____	Inside the New Age Nightmare—Randall Baer	9.99 _____
_____	*A Jewish Conservative Looks at Pagan America—Don Feder	9.99/19.99 _____
_____	Journey Into Darkness—Stephen Arrington	9.99 _____
_____	Kinsey, Sex and Fraud—Dr. Judith A. Reisman/ Edward Eichel	11.99 _____
_____	Legend of the Holy Lance (A Novel)—William T. Still	8.99/16.99 _____
_____	*Loyal Opposition—John Eidsmoe	8.99 _____
_____	New World Order—William T. Still	9.99 _____
_____	One Year to a College Degree—Lynette Long/Eileen Hershberger	9.99 _____
_____	Political Correctness—David Thibodaux	9.99 _____
_____	*Prescription Death—Dr. Reed Bell/Frank York	9.99 _____
_____	*Real Men—Dr. Harold Voth	9.99 _____
_____	"Soft Porn" Plays Hardball—Dr. Judith A. Reisman	8.99/16.95 _____
_____	*Subtle Serpent—Darylann Whitemarsh & Bill Reisman	9.99 _____
_____	To Grow By Storybook Readers—Janet Friend	44.95 per set _____
_____	*Trojan Horse—Brenda Scott & Samantha Smith	9.99 _____
_____	Twisted Cross—Joseph Carr	9.99 _____
_____	*When the Wicked Seize a City—Chuck & Donna McIlhenny/Frank York	9.99 _____
_____	*Why Does a Nice Guy Like Me Keep Getting Thrown in Jail—Randall Terry	8.95 _____
_____	You Hit Like a Girl—Elsa Houtz & William J. Ferkile	9.99 _____

*New Title   **Total** _____
Shipping and Handling _____

AVAILABLE AT BOOKSTORES EVERYWHERE or order direct from:
Huntington House Publishers • P.O. Box 53788 • Lafayette, LA 70505
Send check/money order. For faster service use VISA/MASTERCARD
call toll-free 1-800-749-4009.
Add: Freight and handling, $3.50 for the first book ordered, and $.50 for each additional
book up to 5 books.

Enclosed is $_____ including postage.
VISA/MASTERCARD#_____ Exp. Date_____
Name_____ Phone: ( )_____
Address_____
City, State, Zip_____